STRENGTH HONOR
GL

What people are saying about ...

The Rest *of* Your Story

"Greg is an incredibly gifted thinker and teacher, but grace isn't best understood through explanation. Instead, grace is best understood through experience. It's Greg's story alongside of his teaching that makes this book so powerful. His thoughtfulness and vulnerability will expand your appreciation of grace and help you experience it more deeply yourself. As a personal friend, I've watched how God's grace has healed Greg from shame and despair and set him on a path of redemption and restoration that is filled with joy and freedom. Read this book and let that be true of the rest of your story."

Kyle Idleman, senior pastor at Southeast Christian Church and bestselling author of *Not a Fan*

"Everyone blows it. Few men fully recover and transform the rubble of their broken lives into an unshakable foundation of wholeheartedness. Greg is one of these men. Greg lives to rescue because he's a man who has been rescued. I've had the joy and honor of walking with him enough to know that what he writes is what he preaches. And what he preaches is what he lives. With brutal honesty and compelling vulnerability, he offers a practical and powerful path to recover a life that is truly life. If you or someone you love has been harmed or disenfranchised by religious people yet hold on to a pocket of hope that the life you are searching for is hidden deep within the heart of God, this book is meant for you."

Morgan Snyder, author of *Becoming a King*, founder of BecomeGoodSoil.com, and vice president of Wild at Heart

"I've watched Greg live out the message of this book the past fifteen years with passion and integrity. He's the real deal. In *The Rest of Your Story*, he shares with compelling honesty how, after failure, he rebuilt his life into something real and beautiful. He shows how you can go after God's best for your life as well. Read this and share it with friends. It is a message of hope we all need!"

Jud Wilhite, senior pastor at Central Church and author of *Pursued*

"*The Rest of Your Story* is filled with raw emotions, real relatable stories, and life-changing applications. Greg Lindsey takes you on a journey ... a journey of the heart. In many ways, we all can relate to the emptiness, the hurt, and the hang-ups that he speaks about in this book. If you are looking for something different, something that takes you from pain to living the best life God created you to live, then this is the book for you."

Renee Beebe, executive director of Crossfire Ministries

"As I have come to know Greg Lindsey, he is the real deal! The story of his life is not without pain and choices he regrets. But in the journey of his personal integrity, he wasted no pain in owning his story, experiencing the real Jesus, and returning to the mission of his life of rescuing others. His story makes us all better men."

Bart Hansen, founding board member of Wild at Heart

"*The Rest of Your Story* captures you from the first page. With humility, self-awareness, and God's guidance, Greg discusses difficult issues we all face with personal accountability, conviction, inspiration, and most importantly hope. You will buy copies of this book to give to others to change their lives too."

Jack Briggs, Maj Gen (Ret), EdD, president
and CEO of Springs Rescue Mission

"In this book, Greg Lindsey has written a compelling masterpiece of redemption, hope, and an authentic reminder that our painful life stories really do have a mission attached to them. I know Greg personally and he genuinely lives his message of loving broken and hurting people to restoration, especially those who have been disillusioned with the church as a whole. This book is a must-read! You will be inspired, challenged, and courageously strengthened that there is hope in the rest of your story."

Dr. MelindaJoy Mingo, author of *The Colors of Culture* and *Devotions from the Bus Station*

"I have always admired Greg's ability to weave his own story together and the bigger story of God's kingdom with grace and compassion. This is an invitation for the rest of us to do the same. His words and stories invite all of us into the grand adventure of discovering that story, regardless of how deep our mistakes or glorious our successes."

Stu Davis, executive director of COSILoveYou

"Greg is a man of action, allergic to the status quo. It won't take long to be captured by his shocking authenticity and raw obedience. Greg's story is about a life that every human being longs for but is often either unaware of or unwilling to pursue. This book will solve one of those problems; the other, well, it is up to you to follow Greg down the path to the life you've always wanted."

Roy Moran, senior pastor at Shoal Creek Church and author of *Spent Matches*

"Like Pastor Greg, I grew up being taught how a 'good Christian' should behave to fit into a cultural church box. It is so good to know that instead, the real Christian life involves a daily struggle with our enemy and a decision to fight. Thanks to a God who is all truth and all grace, we ultimately prevail. Please count me in as one of the misfits in God's army!"

Kevin Butcher, president and CEO of Strata Group

"With refreshing transparency, Pastor Greg Lindsey does a masterful job in this book of laying out the journey to health by sharing his testimony of restoration. Every leader needs this book. Greg's clear writing style and brutal honesty are so refreshing in the religious world of 'fake it till you make it,' which doesn't work by the way. I am grateful to have gotten to know Greg and am better for it. I wholeheartedly endorse this book about his story of God's incredible graciousness in his life."

Rev. Jamie Englehart, author and overseer of CIM Network
of Churches and Ministries New Albany, Indiana

"*The Rest of Your Story* offers an authentic, up-close experience of life, church, and Christians (the full spectrum) and an invitation for what the church—what we, you—can be. My hope is the words of this story cause you to pause, rethink, reframe, and remember that you are a 'beloved child that has nothing to prove.' I long for us Christians to see ourselves clearly so we may see others clearly, as our generous Father does. This book will graciously lead you into both spaces."

Abbey Mobolade, mother, nurse, educator,
advocate, and first lady of Colorado Springs

"The path Greg describes is real, available, and worth the risk. It will be far from easy but more than worth it. The words in this book and the man who authored them are helping write a better rest of my story. What about yours? Read the book. Give it to your friends. Gather around a coffee table or a campfire and have real, honest, and open conversations. Your story is still being written, and the best can truly be yet to come."

Terry Anderson, chief operations officer
of Springs Rescue Mission

"Absolutely transformative! Through exceptional vulnerability, authenticity, and encouragement, Lindsey inspires the reader on how discovering your story, experiencing Jesus, and living to rescue can lead to the life God intends for us all. Not as an apathetic, consumeristic Christian, but as a rescue-minded disciple living with vital purpose. Truly life-changing potential!"

Jared McGowen, PhD, Maj, US Army, former Green Beret

"To witness a life, marriage, family, and calling restored is a holy and glorious thing. I had the honor of watching some of this story of rescue unfold. As Greg shares, it did not happen overnight. It took time and grace, along with immense honesty, courage, and humility to fight for the beauty that we now see with him and his family. Seeing his critical need for God and seeking the wisdom and counsel of a few fellow sojourners are the cornerstones of this amazing story of a rescued heart."

Lori McConnell, friend, wife of kingdom
hero and legend Craig McConnell

"I highly recommend that you read Greg's story, which mirrors my story and many others in so many respects. It's a story of brokenness and redemption. It will give you hope that God is good and has your best interests at heart. We can keep getting up after our failures because forgiveness and grace are the cornerstones of the gospel message."

Vance F. Brown, cofounder and executive elder
of Thrivers Leadership Institute and cofounder
and chairman of Exponential Impact

"Pastor Greg has experienced the unconditional and generous act of God's kindness and mercy. He leads the world to Jesus Christ by understanding that the human condition requires compassion and empathy. An excellent reading of God's transformative power of divine grace. It's truly a story of God's love for all people regardless of their actions, beliefs, or status."

Ben Anderson, pastor at Solid Rock Christian Center and executive
director of Solid Rock Community Development Corporation

"*The Rest of Your Story* is for all of us who have been tumbled by our humanity and hunger for authenticity both in our own lives and in that of the church. Greg masterfully points us to the beauty of being rescued by Jesus and being 'alive to rescue' others."

Jon Petersen, president of CityTable and author

"My friend Greg's new book is a fresh and vulnerable journey through redemption, turning personal stories into kingdom lessons of hope and freedom. Engaging and heartfelt, it's more than just another read—it's a transformative experience where each page of his story brings you closer to finding God in your own story."

Daniel Rolfe, senior pastor of Mountain Springs Church

"Greg's vulnerability in this book is a testament of how God uses our flaws and missteps to realize God's love, forgiveness, and safety in him. As our charge is to bring others to Christ, this book reminds us that judgment and condemnation by Christians does not work. A must-read."

Johnna Reeder Kleymeyer, president and CEO of Colorado Springs Chamber of Commerce and Economic Development Corporation

"Greg Lindsey invites us into many raw, real moments of his journey that help us see how important it is to live within three critical, life-altering circles. It's a game changer for the Christian faith and can help us rise up and become the rescuers and warriors that God has called us to be!"

Rebecca Greer, children's ministry director at Discovery Church Colorado

"The only people I trust are those who have been somewhere I don't want to go. Greg has been there, and God has brought him back to guide us into our best story. This is a book from and for the true seeker. Please start over and start here."

Hugh Halter, author of *Brave Cities*, *The Tangible Kingdom*, and *Flesh*

"More than just another Christian book, *The Rest of Your Story* is a much-needed guide for navigating the contours of your life. Greg is skilled at doing this ... I should know, because he's been a consistent friend who has inspired me to trust Jesus during both my good and bad seasons. Now, he's offering to do the same for you."

Caleb Kaltenbach, research pastor at Shepherd Church, founder of The Messy Grace Group, and author of *Messy Grace* and *Messy Truth*

"Pastor Greg validates the pain and hurt many of us have experienced from the greater church. The bold way he shares his personal journey is disruptive and gracious. He invites us to let God transform our pain into a life-giving rescue for others. If you are ready for a comeback, this book is for you!"

Bryan Byrd, fire leader at Wild Courage

"Through his willingness to be vulnerable with his own story, Greg reminds us God's grace extends to all, including those bruised and battered as a result of their own choices. He tops it off with a daring and compelling vision of a dangerous militia—a church fully engaged in the kingdom call to action. A must-read!"

Eric Smith, PhD, partner with One Eleven Capital Group and founder of The Pillar Seminary for Contextual Leadership

"Greg Lindsey's new book, *The Rest of Your Story*, is both inspirational and challenging. I've known Greg for over forty years and was thrilled years ago when he decided to leave his law practice and enter ministry. Today, I'm proud of the way he has bounced back from failure and been restored to a very effective ministry leading a dynamic, healthy church. Greg's transparency about his own mistakes lifts our spirits by reminding us God uses imperfect people—and that means God can use every one of us!"

Bob Russell, retired senior minister of Southeast Christian Church, Louisville, KY

"*The Rest of Your Story* is a breath of fresh air for those who have wondered why they have not found the fulfillment they were looking for in their Christian faith. This book brings things back to proper focus. Christianity is about Jesus, and Jesus loves us for who we are, period, regardless of our flaws, mistakes, and especially our sins. If you are looking for a book that shows you how to live your full potential as a Christian through Jesus, despite flaws or mistakes, read this book today."

Jason Redman, US Navy SEAL (ret.), *New York Times* bestselling author of *The Trident* and *Overcome*

"Greg Lindsey has always struck me as an authentic and down-to-earth leader in a world where authenticity can be hard to find. He's not chasing fame or the spotlight; he's a genuine servant who has experienced the transformative power of grace. His book delves deep into the intricacies of the human journey, celebrating our vulnerabilities while highlighting the relentless pursuit of personal growth. It offers readers a priceless roadmap for healing and rediscovering their life's purpose. This book is a must-read for anyone on the path to genuine restoration and meaningful transformation."

Justin Knapp, CEO of SpaceTogether

"Part memoir, part spiritual, the rest of Greg's story moves beyond crashing and burning to a story of an encounter with Jesus' rescue and living to rescue others. Greg is honest and vulnerable, and he is quick to give credit to others who have supported him along the way, including his wife, Stacy, whom he calls one of the real heroes of his story. And still, he concludes that the *hero* is you, as there is no limit to what Jesus can do with and through the rest of your story. I highly recommend this book; I had a hard time putting it down once I started reading."

Yemi Mobolade, former pastor and current mayor of Colorado Springs

The Rest
of Your Story

The Path to the Christian Life You Want

GREG LINDSEY

Foreword by JOHN ELDREDGE

transforming lives together

THE REST OF YOUR STORY
Published by David C Cook
4050 Lee Vance Drive
Colorado Springs, CO 80918 U.S.A.

Integrity Music Limited, a Division of David C Cook
Brighton, East Sussex BN1 2RE, England

DAVID C COOK® and related marks are registered trademarks of David C Cook.

Unless otherwise noted, all Scripture quotations are taken from the Holy Bible,
New International Version®, NIV®. Copyright © 1973, 2011 by Biblica, Inc.™ Used
by permission of Zondervan. All rights reserved worldwide. www.zondervan.
com. The "NIV" and "New International Version" are trademarks registered in the
United States Patent and Trademark Office by Biblica, Inc.™ Scripture quotations
marked KJV are taken from the King James Version of the Bible. (Public Domain.)

Library of Congress Control Number 2024930358
ISBN 978-0-8307-8582-7
eISBN 978-0-8307-8583-4

© 2024 Gregory A. Lindsey

The Team: Michael Covington, Kevin Scott, James Hershberger,
Jack Campbell, Susan Murdock
Cover Design: Joe Cavazos
Cover Image: Martino Pietropoli_Unsplash
Interior "GL" Logo and Circles Graphics: Keith Locke
Cover Author Bio Photo: Ashley Brunt

Printed in the United States of America
First Edition 2024

1 2 3 4 5 6 7 8 9 10

021124

To my wife, Stacy, and our daughters, Sydney, Sloane,
Spencer, and Stella. Your beauty, strength, and grace
continue to astonish me and change the world.

Contents

Foreword   17

Introduction: Head-on Collision   19

PART ONE: DISCOVER YOUR STORY

Chapter 1: But I Still Haven't Found What I'm Looking For   27

Chapter 2: Point of Origin   39

Chapter 3: The Only Easy Day Was Yesterday   51

Chapter 4: Buried Treasure   65

PART TWO: EXPERIENCE JESUS

Chapter 5: Why Church and Religion Don't Work   81

Chapter 6: Something to Prove   95

Chapter 7: The Rest of the Story   107

Chapter 8: Different   123

PART THREE: LIVE TO RESCUE

Chapter 9: Embracing Unconventional You   143

Chapter 10: Finding Tonto   153

Chapter 11: A Call to Action with a Sense of Urgency   169

Chapter 12: A Dangerous Militia   183

A Note from Stacy   197

Acknowledgments   201

Notes   205

Foreword

Look—I know. We've all had so many helpings of "Your life can be great!" sermons and podcasts, and way too many slices of let's-get-real "authenticity" that it's made us nauseous. Some of us tried hard to combine the two, because we were told it would change our lives. But nothing really happened. And nothing really seemed to happen in the lives and characters of the folks selling us the programs.

No wonder so many people are giving up on God and the Christian faith. It just looks like lap after lap around the carousel.

So here comes along yet another book offering hope and change—and by a pastor, to make things worse. I feel jaded myself.

But I've put my name on the cover, so allow me to explain why.

The "authenticity" movement in the church failed because people didn't have anything to be authentic about beyond their mess. To "be real" was synonymous with being broken. Only broken. No one was in front of us living out a way *through* our pain to something genuinely wonderful. Honestly—far more people have found help in a therapist's office than they ever have in church.

Authenticity stuck in brokenness isn't helpful; it's depressing.

Meanwhile, the "Your life can be great!" buffet of Christian promises grew rank because while leaders talked a lot *about* God and *about* his promises, over time, it didn't seem like they actually *knew* God and *experienced* his promises. Loads and loads of shiny content, very little actual transformation.

Right?

All I can tell you is this: There are good leaders who actually know and experience God. They have some authority to talk about transformation because they first chose to live it out themselves before they preached on it. Greg Lindsey is one of those leaders.

His church actually helps people move from *only broken* to *broken but becoming whole* and even on to *mostly whole*. Within a Christian framework. Better still, *because* of the Christian framework.

God is real, and available, and wonderful.

Your story matters to him, and the rest of your story can be better than what has been *because* God is real, and available, and wonderful.

Interested? Read on.

John Eldredge
Bestselling author
President of Wild at Heart

Head-on Collision

"Life is difficult. This is a great truth,
one of the greatest truths."

M. Scott Peck, *The Road Less Traveled*

— ◇ —

I started writing this book sixteen years ago. I didn't get very far. My heart was not in the right place. I was an absolute mess—full of guilt, shame, sorrow, hurt, embarrassment, and anger. I was locked and loaded, ready to go off on every Christian who would listen to me. Now, I'm a different man. I've learned a lot. Thank God for that.

It wasn't until I blew my own life up that I realized something had been missing in my version of Christianity. Looking back, my former religious Christian life didn't work. It felt empty, flat, and not even remotely close to the abundant life Jesus said is available to us. My

Christianity was missing something, as if I was working from a bad or incomplete definition of the Christian life. The catalyst that helped me recognize that was also the very worst moment of my life. A horrible Friday night, eighteen years ago, changed everything in my life.

After sitting in my car for several minutes, I finally staggered into the house. I wasn't drunk or under the influence of any substance, but I was carrying overwhelming guilt, shame, and fear. *How could I have done this? I've betrayed so many people, especially those who love and trust me most—my wife, Stacy, and our four daughters. My life is over.*

Entering the house, I did my best to fake it with my family and then disappeared into my home office. Setting my backpack on the floor, I noticed an envelope on my chair. It was Stacy's handwriting. My heart pounded in my chest, I felt sick to my stomach, and I began to sweat as I inched closer to the note. Finally, I could read what was written on the envelope: "To the man I am so proud to call my husband." I sank into my chair and wept. She didn't know. In a few short hours her entire world would come crashing down.

We had met in the seventh grade, started dating in high school, and married when we were twenty. Married for twenty-one years, we now had four beautiful daughters, ages fourteen, eleven, six, and four. Stacy had been in management at a Fortune 500 company, and I was a trial attorney when, together, we decided to move to North Carolina to start and lead a new church plant. It was a new and completely different life for us, a life that we absolutely loved. It was not just a job for me; I had found my calling, what God created me to do. Almost three years had passed since then, and the church was thriving. It was everything we had hoped and dreamed it could be and more.

As I sat in my home office, my mind raced. Just an hour earlier, I had resigned as lead pastor of a fast-growing church of six hundred. Surely this was all a terrible nightmare. We had worked so hard and absolutely loved our lives, and in one selfish instant I had taken it all away. I had been caught in an affair with someone in the church. I was unfaithful to Stacy. Like most couples, we had experienced ups and downs in our marriage. Most of the downs were on me. There had been other brutal mistakes, screwups, failures, and challenges in my past before ministry, but the past decade had been amazing for us. The next decade—and those to follow—would surely be hell.

All I could hear ringing in my ears were two words—*how* and *why*. How could this have happened? Why did I do it? The most terrifying part for me, other than the prospect of life without my family, was that I didn't know how to answer those two questions. Stacy's note read, "Thank you for who you are," and in that moment I had no idea who I was. Two days later, as I was cleaning out my office at the church, a leader in the church told me, "You had better watch yourself, Greg. You are outside the grace of God." Honestly, I knew better, but at that moment, I believed him. It would take me a while to recover from that encounter.

Almost nineteen years have passed since that terrible, gut-wrenching Friday night. Fortunately, my family is still intact, thriving, and better than ever, thanks to God's grace and my incredible wife. You don't have to just take my word for it. Flip to the end of the book and read Stacy's perspective on the story. We now have three sons-in-law, three grandsons, four granddaughters, and a ten-year-old black Lab named Bentley. I am always quick to give credit to the two real heroes in the story—Jesus and Stacy. Most wives would have done the expected thing and called it quits. Many, including those in the church, encouraged Stacy to do just that. I'm forever grateful that she didn't. Instead, despite being criticized for it, she decided to wait and see how my counseling went. Since then, she has traveled this journey with me at the expense of public embarrassment, humiliation, abandonment by "friends," and lots of church hurt. Stacy is the greatest gift God has given me on this earth. Her willingness to travel the brutal road less traveled has helped thousands of people find hope, life, healing, redemption, and freedom.

As you might imagine, when the sh-tuff hit the fan in my life, people, especially church people, couldn't distance themselves fast enough. Having been in church my whole life, I've observed that this is what we do. At forty-one, my world grew as quiet, dark, and lonely as it had ever been. In that desert—that quiet, that darkness, that loneliness, that hopelessness—with the help of a great counselor and friend, I found the life I had been looking for as long as I could remember. In my very worst moment, God began to show me a different path.

After spending over two thousand weekends of my life in church, attending Christian schools, memorizing Bible verses and worship songs, becoming a pastor, and generally checking all the Christian boxes, I had still missed out on experiencing the abundant life Jesus offers. Most of us do. But I want something different for you.

I'm not blaming any church or pastor for my failures. But I am suggesting that we have a huge problem in the American church. We must get to the bottom of this. The abundant life Jesus came to bring is available to us. Meanwhile, some real nasty religious junk prevents us from finding it. This problem can't be fixed by coming up with a new, cool, dope, hip, or rad approach. We must get back to what Jesus intended this life to be.

After I was in the desert about three years, despite the critics, God restored me to ministry. Ever since, I have been leading a church in Colorado, a messy yet safe place for all people, regardless of how their stories read or what they do or don't believe.

In an instant, I saw my life go from the best to the worst. While I never saw it coming, it was my own doing. My own story got the best of me. It can happen to anyone. In one way or another, it happens to everyone. While we clearly understand the significance of sin, we fail to understand the significance of our stories. And it's time for that to change. It must change. The answers you seek are right in front of you, my friend. That is why I am writing this book. The answers you need are found in the rest of your story.

It took a total collapse, betraying the trust of others, deeply hurting those I love the most, embarrassing those who believed in me, and public shame and humiliation to open my eyes to the most important lessons I have ever learned in my life. Yes, I take total responsibility for all that I have done in my life, but it was a head-on collision that I never saw coming and almost cost me everything that ultimately led me to the life I had always desired. If sharing my experience can help you avoid the pain that I and those closest to me have endured, it will have been worth it.

For most of us, there is a significant gap between the life we are living and the life we want. Let's go on a journey together to change that! Maybe you have determined that you want nothing to do with the Christian life because of what you have experienced. I get it, but what if this path is different? What if it leads to a different place than where many who call themselves Christian have settled? The road we are looking for is actually right in front of us. Unfortunately, most of us miss it. My purpose is to help you find it. The journey may be strenuous and difficult at times, but it promises to be exhilarating. Stay curious and take risks, my friend. There's hope. I promise you will never look back.

Greg Lindsey
Colorado Springs, CO
April 2023

Part One

Discover Your Story

But I Still Haven't Found What I'm Looking For

"Success is never final and failure is never fatal."
John Wooden

*"The mass of men lead lives
of quiet desperation."*
Henry David Thoreau

—◆—

One summer, my second daughter, Sloane, then thirteen years old, came home from a basketball camp at the University of North Carolina Wilmington wearing a camp shirt that said "Success is never final and failure is never fatal." This quote from legendary coach John Wooden could not have come at a better time for me. Just two years before, I had crashed and burned as a pastor in a very public, embarrassing, and humiliating way. My failure certainly seemed fatal.

Many Christians told me it was over for me. They said I would never be in ministry again and that, if I tried, God would not bless it. Now, I'm not bashing Christians. Christians can be some of the most awesome people in the world—when we get it right. Unfortunately, we often don't.

Thankfully, in my failure, God showed up for me and began to teach me about myself and what life with him could really be. He has continued to do that these past nineteen years. Before, I was working from a bad, incomplete definition of *Christian*. As a result, I had still not found what I was looking for.

Maybe you are beginning to wonder if this book is only for those who are attempting a comeback after screwing up their lives. It's not. It includes that, yes, but is so much more than that. Achieving success as the world defines it often leaves even many "successful people" feeling empty inside. No matter how successful or great your life may be right now, you may still be longing for something more. There is likely a part of you that still wonders, *Is this it?*

When the new church plant in North Carolina was less than a year old, a pastor in Washington, DC, contacted me about a one-day leadership conference for about four to five hundred leaders in his church. He invited me and three other church-planting pastors to tell our stories. I remember thinking, *Here we go. This is what I have been looking for my entire life. Finally, I'm there. I have arrived.* A few months later, I flew to DC, excited for the conference. After a Friday night dinner, Saturday was go time. I had a blast sharing what God was doing in our new church plant, as well as hearing from the other three church planters. It was a great day.

When it was over, someone took me to the airport so I could get home to preach the next morning. Shortly after takeoff, as I reflected on my experience that day, an uneasiness came over me that I couldn't shake. When the "fasten seat belts" sign went off, rather than reviewing my sermon notes as planned, I sat paralyzed in the darkness. Where was the high I had felt only a few hours before? I thought about the other church planters I had hung out with that day, all three of them awesome guys doing awesome kingdom work. Then, I realized where the uneasiness and discouragement were coming from. While we were all doing similar things, each of them seemed to have something I felt was missing in my own life and story. They radiated peace, joy, happiness, contentment, and freedom that I knew I still had not found. I had found my calling. I knew who I was created to be—and yet, something was still missing. Even as a pastor leading a successful, growing church, I still hadn't found what I was looking for. It was only a few months later that I blew up my life.

U2's lead singer, Bono, sang:

> I have climbed the highest mountains
> I have run through the fields ...
> I have run, I have crawled, I have scaled these
>   city walls ...
> But I still haven't found what I'm looking for.

That sounds a lot like the rat race, the quest, the life of quiet desperation, the life that most of us live. My experience is that this is true both inside and outside the church. Maybe for you there is a tension between the life you have and the one you dream of living. Some experience it as a dull ache, while for others it is extreme pain. Either way, it is only when we admit that this tension is present that we can move forward. And yes, it is okay to admit this tension even if you are a follower of Jesus. I know Jesus is supposed to be enough. We will talk about that more in the pages to come. We are *all* desperately looking for more, and too often, we resign ourselves to accepting that our lives are already "as good as they're going to get." But nothing could be further from the truth. There's always more available with Jesus.

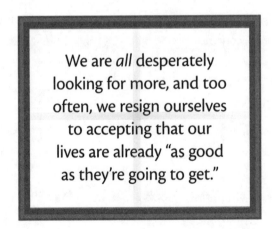

> We are *all* desperately looking for more, and too often, we resign ourselves to accepting that our lives are already "as good as they're going to get."

The answers seem so obvious. If you just make the team, play the right sports, if the right guy or girl says yes, if you graduate from high school, get a great job, get a scholarship, make a certain amount of money, get engaged, get married, live in the right house in the right neighborhood, gain the applause or approval of the right people, wear the right clothes, get in shape, earn a degree, belong to the right clubs, eat at certain restaurants, go to the right church, get religion, have the right friends, go to graduate school, have smart kids, get a promotion, own a boat, have a place in the mountains and at the beach, drive a cool car, become a millionaire or billionaire, then you will have found what you are looking for. Maybe I didn't define your idea of success precisely, but you know what I am talking about.

Most of us set out to find satisfaction by destination. We play the "if only" game. You know how it goes—if only I were married, if only I were CEO, if only I had a million dollars, if only I led a megachurch. We convince ourselves that we will finally be happy and content when a certain event happens. Me too. That's the journey I was on for most of my life. We wrongly assume that a certain destination will bring an end to our searching. We couldn't be more wrong.

The Danger of Unawareness

At my rock bottom, I turned to President Bill Clinton. Maybe that surprises you. Why not Billy Graham, Andy Stanley, Craig Groeschel, or Steven Furtick? At the time, my personal experience with church and Christians ranged somewhere between painful and excruciating. So, it somehow seemed safer to turn to President Clinton's autobiography, *My Life*, to see what he learned from his affair that might benefit me. What I discovered really hit home.

Despite his personal and political success, President Clinton had lived with a nagging, agitating, frustrating sense that something was still missing from his life. It took a highly publicized, thoroughly humiliating moral failure to prompt him to find the source of the feelings that had led him to this dark place. To some extent, this darker, shadow side—including all the insecurities that lie beneath the surface—is present in all our stories. If it is not recognized, understood, faced, and dealt with, it can easily lead to self-destruction. There is grave danger in our unawareness. Christian or not, there is grave danger in overlooking the significance of our own stories.

To find what we are looking for in life, we must first become aware of why we are looking for it. At first, we are blissfully unaware of the significance of our stories—stories that are often reduced to our mistakes, blowups, uh-ohs, "wish I hadn't done thats," the things that we have done to others. We may not even have a category for the things that have been done to us, said to us, and said about us—including all the people, things, moments, and experiences that have shaped us every bit as much as the mistakes we have made. What we are looking for is not a destination; it is not an external, tangible thing. If we still haven't found what we are looking for, despite all our years in church and our very best "Christian" efforts, here it is: we must learn to stop looking *around* and start looking *within*.

My own self-destruction nearly destroyed me and my family. The key word is *nearly*. I hope you find hope in that. Nothing you have done or experienced is irredeemable if you are willing to do the work. Every train wreck in life, every head-on collision, presents a real opportunity. It will take some digging, exploration, and excavation, requiring real effort. It will likely involve some pain too. At times you may be tempted to hit the eject button and abandon the journey altogether. My personal journey over the past nineteen years has been simultaneously one of the most excruciatingly painful and incredibly rewarding and beautiful seasons of my life. All the digging, the excavation, and the pain of the journey into my past ultimately led to the life I had been looking for my entire life. The same can be true of you.

Opportunity in Disaster

As a boy, I loved to go camping. It was especially cool to go camping with my dad. My dad lost his own dad to tuberculosis when he was six years old, had an abusive stepdad, and was later raised by an uncle. His uncle was a good man who had boys of his own and did his best to treat my father like one of his own. But my dad never really had a father. Even so, my dad did the best he could, loved me, and was my best man at my wedding. I will never forget our family camping trips to Otter Creek Park in Kentucky when I was a boy. My dad was always the "fire master." He absolutely loved to build and tend to campfires.

There is something special about a fire and the atmosphere it creates. Imagine sitting by a campfire, laughing over drinks with family and friends. After the last log is burned, the fire dies down, and everyone heads to their tents for the evening. The next morning, you wake up to a pile of ashes. As you grab a stick and poke around in the ash, though, you see a spark and maybe even some hot coals covered by the ashes. It may take some work to get it going again, but the fire isn't really out. It simply needs to be restored. With some effort, the flames can and will burn again.

That's my story. It can be yours too. But it requires poking around in the ashes of your life, taking a journey back into and through your story. Whether you are currently on top of the world, at rock bottom, or somewhere in between, that kind of journey will change your life forever. To get where you want to go and find the life you want to live requires self-awareness, and self-awareness requires us to be in touch with how we feel. I learned that the hard way. I'm inviting you to learn from my mistakes. Despite how kumbaya or touchy-feely this may seem at the moment, I urge you to consider taking this journey with me. The challenge is simple—don't quit, keep reading, and stay on the path. I promise you, as hopeless as it seems, there is a light at the end of your tunnel. This journey leads to the life you want, the life we all want.

What this path requires is commitment to a life of continual self-examination and reflection, daily walking in authenticity and humility with God, and allowing him to reveal the broken places in us, to heal us, redeem us, restore us, and set our broken and captive hearts free so we can experience the life he sent his son, Jesus, to bring us. Most of us, even those of us who have spent our lives in church trying our best to follow Jesus, have only experienced a part of the life that is available to us. The good news is that every single day of our lives, there is more life available in and with Jesus.

The path to the life you want requires you to begin thinking, digging, excavating, exploring, and going places you most likely have never been before. It is a new way of living. I will share lessons I have learned and a strategy that has helped me find peace, joy, hope, freedom, and fulfillment in life. Regardless of where you are right now, you can take your life to a whole new level. What you are looking for is straight ahead. Let's get started—by looking within.

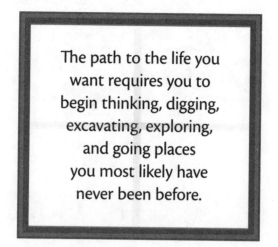

The path to the life you
want requires you to
begin thinking, digging,
excavating, exploring,
and going places
you most likely have
never been before.

Many of us have found church, discovered our sin problem, accepted Jesus, and are believing and behaving the best we know how. We are on a path to eternal life, but we would not describe our daily life as life to the fullest. We may not say this in church (something feels wrong about doing that), but life often feels empty, even with Jesus in it. What if there is another way, another path?

There is, but it's not anything new. Like Jeremiah said, it's an ancient path: "Stand at the crossroads and look; ask for the ancient paths, ask where the good way is, and walk in it, and you will find rest for your souls" (Jer. 6:16). Most of us still haven't found what we are looking for. We are not even sure what it looks like. All the plays we've run from the various church playbooks have landed us nowhere. I'm not suggesting that I have all the answers, but I want to show you something and give you something to think about. What if, instead of the linear path, complete with its list of programs, steps, tips, and techniques, it instead looks a lot more like the following diagram?

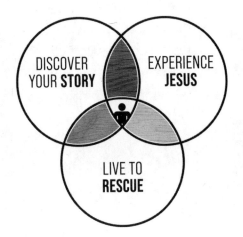

What if, instead of being a linear path, it's organic. We all drift inside of these three circles during our lives. If you are like me, you have drifted completely out of all of them at some point in your life. We all drift around, and that's okay. Life inside these circles is better than life outside. The idea is to keep pulling back to center. The key is all three circles all the time. Most of our church experience places us in two circles, not all three. We have our Jesus experience, and then we get busy with and for Jesus. Nothing wrong with that. It gets us part of the way to the life we all want. What sets the three-circle life apart is the "discover your story" piece. This journey is not primarily about discovering what you've done wrong. It's also about considering what's been done to you and how that has affected you.

What does it look like for us to experience Jesus in all of that? Honestly, it's game-changing, life-changing stuff. It is a path to freedom like few of us have ever experienced. There is so much more that Jesus wants to do, so much more healing, redemption, and restoration that Jesus wants to bring into each of our stories.

Nobody has the market cornered on the life that Jesus came to bring us except Jesus himself. So, I'm not suggesting that this diagram and the life it represents are the be-all/end-all, or that we have it all figured out. I am saying that this is how Jesus rescued me. It is how he saved my marriage, my family, my life, and my ministry. I am saying that thousands of people have found this to be exactly what they have been looking for. It's what they were trying to chase down their entire lives and yet hadn't found or experienced in any church. It has redefined the word *Christian* for them and for me. They are experiencing a Christian life today like they never have before. It is not nearly as much about what we have been taught, what we've read, memorized, quoted, studied, or know, as it is about what we've missed.

Could this be what you're missing? I'm not asking you to agree with me. Let's just continue to take this journey together, talk through it, wrestle with it, and see.

~ 2 ~

Point of Origin

*"Self-awareness touches all the other
disciplines because it is foundational to
every other element of greatness."*

Reggie McNeal

———◇———

As a young state prosecutor in the Commonwealth Attorney's Office in Louisville, Kentucky, I often had the privilege of working with arson detectives. I was always amazed by their ability to locate the point of origin for a fire when all they had to work with was soot and ashes. Sometimes it took a while to find it. But if we were going to understand how the fire occurred, we had to know where it started.

Learning where a fire began is helpful, but it doesn't take away the fire's devastating effects. Wouldn't it be great if we could see the potential fire hazards beneath the surface of our lives before the inevitable destruction occurs? I wish I would have. That's what I want for you. Unfortunately, for most of us, it is only after the devastation and destruction have happened that we begin to examine the source of what went wrong, to ask how and why it could have occurred. By then, pain and destruction are unavoidable. Why not conduct the investigation before the destruction ever begins? We might say that such investigations take time and effort, and we don't really see the need. Things are just fine. But are they?

Here's something we don't often talk about in church. There is real danger in entertaining negative thoughts and feelings, particularly when they are about ourselves. Usually, those closest to us are at the highest risk of serious hurt, heartache, and heartbreak if we allow negative sparks to smolder within us. I did, and it almost cost me everything. Even an optimist like myself can appear optimistic on the surface and still be completely taken out by the power of negative thinking.

Taking Our Thoughts Captive

After I blew up my life and had to leave ministry, I took a job in the mortgage business, which I had learned something about six years earlier while doing real estate closing work as an attorney. A friend who owned a small mortgage company offered me the job. It seemed a good opportunity to support my family while doing the inner work necessary to save my marriage.

I thought I knew sales. After all, I had spent years in the courtroom making the case to juries. But there is a completely different dynamic involved when your income is totally dependent on your ability to make a sale. Little did I know I was coming out of my own self-destruction into the mortgage business during a declining and tightening market. I thought my self-image couldn't get any lower.

Yeah, I was wrong. I was still coming to terms with having thrown a hand grenade into my own living room with my family sitting in it, ripping out their hearts. My actions had crushed and devastated my wife and girls. They were still with me and loved me, and I knew they were working hard trying to forgive me. But it took a lot of time and a whole lot of deep soul work for me to forgive myself. I carried it with me everywhere. Meanwhile, I had to try to pull myself together, smile for realtors and referral sources, and try to earn a living for my family.

As I wrestled with all of that, I couldn't help but think of Coach Rick Pitino. You may be thinking, *President Clinton and Coach Pitino? Where's Jesus in all of this?* Stay with me, we are almost there. I had read Coach Pitino's book *Success Is a Choice* several years earlier but picked it up again as I struggled to make it in the mortgage business and support my family. About midway through the book, I zeroed in on this poignant quote: "It requires discipline to keep fighting off those negative viruses that always will be swirling around you."[1]

I put the book down to give this some thought. I had spent my whole life in church but never once considered the negative voices, messages, agreements, and "viruses" swirling around me nonstop. Coach Pitino suggested I address those negative thoughts I had ignored for so long—which was something I had never heard or thought about in forty-plus years of church. It would require discipline and introspection for me not only to focus on what I had done but to analyze the thoughts and feelings beneath those actions. This experience gave the "power of the negative" a whole new meaning to me. I realized that we must appreciate the destruction that negative thinking can lead to in our lives. Left unattended, just like small sparks can grow into giant fires, small thoughts can quickly develop into huge problems in our lives. In my experience, despite being told to take our thoughts captive in 2 Corinthians 10, we Christians don't give this much thought. We aren't really taught to do that. Having grown up in church, the only thoughts I believed I should pay attention to were the tempting and sinful thoughts in my life. Counseling began to help me with this.

Having said that, my counseling journey didn't get off to a great start. The unhelpful church leader I mentioned before appointed himself to decide which counselor I would see—a friend he liked to mountain bike with. He told me that his friend was exactly what I needed because I needed a counselor who would not like me.

So, I saw his counselor and quickly discovered the church leader was right. The guy did not like me, and I had absolutely no problem disliking him back. It was disappointing for me because I knew I needed help. My marriage was hanging by a thin thread, and every single day mattered. After two meetings with this counselor, I felt deeply discouraged. I was paying him money I couldn't afford, and it seemed to me that we had made zero progress. I remember thinking, *Dude, I have a marriage that is falling apart by the minute, and you want me to try to remember my childhood?* That, in addition to his complete lack of kindness and compassion, had me feeling so hope-less. I wanted to be done with him, but I knew I couldn't walk away. Then God showed up.

I remember that Sunday afternoon like it was yesterday. I was scheduled for my third visit the next morning and was totally dejected about that. Then, I received a call from his wife. She said she was sorry but that the counselor had been in a boating accident and would not be able to see clients for several months. I responded that I was "sorry" to hear that while I proceeded to do a happy dance in the family room of our home. Thank you, Jesus! I realize that Jesus didn't cause the accident to happen, but we can still praise him when he doesn't cause such an event. I wasn't praising him that my counselor was hurt (I'm not the sharpest pencil in the box, but sharp enough to know not to do that). I was praising him for the fact I didn't have to see that guy ever again.

I haven't seen him since. Praise Jesus! Long story short, I was referred to a new counselor named Rob who would forever change the trajectory of my life. Having said that, though, guess where Rob wanted to start? You guessed it. Back as far as I could remember, in my childhood. I was pissed and voiced my objection to Rob, stressing that my marriage desperately needed help. He explained that noth-ing would affect my marriage more than the journey that he wanted to take with me. If there was any hope for my marriage, this journey was required. All of that to say, I still didn't get it. Let's be honest, counseling is often seen as something that only really messed-up people do, something that real Christians shouldn't need, and some-thing that we hide in the church. We couldn't be more wrong.

> Counseling is often seen as something that only really messed-up people do, something that real Christians shouldn't need, and something that we hide in the church. We couldn't be more wrong.

Rob also liked to ask, "How do you feel?" It's a question that never seemed relevant in my life. What difference does it really make? Rub some dirt on it, and get over it and on with it. I never understood the importance of this question. I do now. It's actually a very important question.

Having said that, here's one that is even more important: "How do you feel about yourself? What do you think and how do you feel when you look in the mirror?" You need to go beyond your education, résumé, job, and the value of your stock portfolio. You even need to go beyond how your spouse and others feel about you. What do you think about the man or woman in the mirror? How do you really feel about that person?

Let's take one more step into this. Perhaps this is even a better question: "What would those who are closest to you think of you if they knew everything that you know about you?" Now that's a little scary, isn't it? Especially in and around church and church people! We will talk more about that later.

There is something about how masculinity is viewed, something about being a man in our culture, that tells a guy that he is not supposed to feel and that feelings don't really matter. From the time we are little guys, we are told "get up, suck it up, you are not hurt." As I think more about it, it isn't just a guy thing. As my four daughters were growing up, I am not proud of this, but I would sometimes give them the same message. The bottom line is that we tend to grow up out of touch with how we feel. We may know that something is not right, but we can't really define it or wrap our heads around it. All the while, we are taught to take the punch and not let anyone know we are hurt. We let it go, and yet, the feelings don't go away. They get stronger. And when we have negative feelings and we are not able to identify the thoughts that are causing them, our default mechanism is to do something to make ourselves feel better. What we turn to may be terribly self-destructive. That's my story.

More Than What You've Done

I grew up the skinny redheaded kid. I wish I had a dollar for every time I heard "I'd rather be dead than red on the head" and for every fight I got into because of it. My hair was also very short for most of my years growing up. My dad had a short burr and thought, much to my horror, that I needed one too. That might have been okay in the 1950s. It wasn't exactly in style when I was growing up. I remember one summer evening when I was about thirteen years old. I was playing in a Little League baseball game and had just hit a double, safely sliding into second base. As I slid, my helmet came off, exposing my freshly cut (shaved) hair. I put my helmet back on and assumed the position leading off from second base. As I stood there, ready to steal, the opposing shortstop said, "Where in the world did you get that haircut, boy?" A fight ensued—actually more of a wrestling match, I think. I don't remember who won or if a winner could even be declared. I do know that he hit a nerve. It really pissed me off. I thought my hair made me less than desirable to look at. This led to all kinds of negative feelings about myself. My response was not nearly as much about what he said as it was about how what he said made me feel about myself. It would take me about thirty more years to figure that out. I thought I was simply being a man.

We will have a larger discussion about this in the next chapter, but let me quickly say this. These things happen every day in every one of our lives and stories. Each of us has an enemy who has not been simply tempting us to screw up and sin. Since the moment we were born, he has been building a case to keep us from seeing ourselves as God sees us. His negative chatter is constant. He is an accuser, a liar, and the father of lies, constantly reminding us of what we have done and what has been done to, said to, and said about us. Over the course of time, these small negative thoughts and messages are solidified as facts, conclusions, and agreements, which can lead to huge problems in our lives. This is not merely about the power of positive thinking. Most of us fail to understand the significance of our own negative thinking. The rest of our stories are killing us, and we don't even know it.

I wasn't aware of the many negative self-concepts and thoughts I had accumulated over the course of my life that were causing me to feel terrible about myself. Being a pastor was not an antidote for that. I felt that I didn't measure up; that I wasn't good looking enough, strong enough, tough enough; that I didn't have and would never have what it takes to be a man. I didn't know what to do with that. No one told me that it mattered. *Just rub some dirt on it. You're okay. You'll be fine.* So, rather than identifying the messages and agreements, taking them to God, and receiving the healing I needed, I developed a defense mechanism of my own. If I couldn't make the pain go away, I would medicate it or at least compensate for it. That became the central theme of the first forty years or so of my life, even as a pastor.

When negative feelings came, I ran the other direction, driving to achieve and seeking affirmation in an attempt to soothe the wounds and the pain. I wasn't even aware that I was doing it. I used achievement to compensate for my own negative thoughts and self-image. In the end, it wasn't enough. It never is. Most of us unknowingly allow negative thoughts to drive our lives. They are an unbelievably powerful part of each of our stories. We must stop ignoring them. They are keeping us from the path that leads to the life we all want. As we let them go unnoticed and unaddressed, we will continue to miss the path.

The first step on this journey is to look deep within ourselves. We must discover the point of origin. That begins with a journey into the past—a journey that most of us have little interest in taking. Most of us have spent our entire lives trying to forget that stuff, put it behind us, or convince ourselves that it didn't matter or it didn't hurt. We have spent a considerable amount of time trying to bury it. Why in the world would we dig it back up now? The truth is that most of us would rather take another path. Not only that, we have been taught, trained, and conditioned to take another path. But the "Christian" path of believing the right things and behaving the right way will never lead any of us to the life we want. It's about so much more than managing our sin. We must understand the significance of our stories.

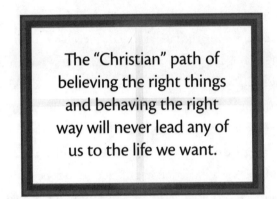

The "Christian" path of believing the right things and behaving the right way will never lead any of us to the life we want.

When I blew up my life, the response of most church people was quite simple: you have a sin issue. I was a sex addict and probably addicted to pornography. Guess what? Neither of those things was true. Don't hear me wrong. I am not minimizing my sin or our sin; I am aware of its seriousness and all that the Bible has to say about it. We are all hopeless without the blood, cross, and forgiveness of Jesus, period. I have needed Jesus' forgiveness in my life more than most people I know.

Own It

When we look within, we tend to take a journey to and through our sin and over and around our stories. Having been taught to have an intense focus on what we've done, we often never consider what might be an even more important question: Why do we do it? Because we are just born that way? Because we are all sinners and on our own fall short of the glory of God like Paul said in the book of Romans? That's true. I'm not contradicting Paul, but there's so much more to it than that.

I love this Brené Brown quote that sits framed on the table next to where I sit early each morning: "Owning our story and loving ourselves through that process is the bravest thing that we'll ever do." It takes courage to confess, but even more to dig for the point of origin of our problem. Brené Brown is right. Bravery is found in owning our stories—the whole story. Yes, of course, this includes all that we have done, but it also includes all that has been done to, said to, and said about us. It involves learning to love ourselves despite the messages that have left us feeling unlovable. Learning how to invite Jesus into all that mess and allow him to love us through it—and heal us, redeem us, and restore us—is even more important.

We will talk more about that in the next section. For now, let's settle on this. Despite our best attempts, we cannot believe, behave, or serve ourselves to the life that we want.

Most of us spend our lives treating symptoms and never really getting to the source. We spend our time, energy, and effort focused on the mistakes we have made and trying to make that right, rather than doing the real work of digging into the why behind what we have done. There is so much more to it than "we were tempted and failed." The path to real purpose in our lives requires a journey through our pain. In fact, good luck finding and living out your purpose if you haven't taken a journey through all the pain in your life.

Richard Rohr said it this way: "If we do not transform our pain, we will most assuredly transmit it."[2] That may be one of the most powerful quotes you will ever hear. You should probably pause right now and write that one down. Being transformed by the renewing of our minds (Rom. 12) requires much more than simply learning to eliminate our sinful thoughts. We do not live our lives in a vacuum. It all starts with us recognizing what we are up against.

— 3 —

The Only Easy Day
Was Yesterday

"You can't fight a battle you don't think exists."

John Eldredge

❖

I love the military. My dad served in General George Patton's Third Army in World War II. I grew up hearing stories about foxholes in France, which ultimately led me to Officer Candidate School (OCS) in the United States Marine Corps at Quantico, Virginia, in the summer of 1985. I have always had mad respect for all in our military, but especially for those in the Special Operations community. It has been a blast not only to read everything I can get my hands on but to actually meet and become friends with some who have served or are currently serving in Special Operations. Years ago, I stumbled across a motto of the US Navy SEALs that immediately resonated with me on a deep level: "The only easy day was yesterday." In other words, every day is a battle. It is never easy. I connected so strongly with that message because it was consistent with what life with Jesus had become and was continuing to become for me. The abundant life Jesus came to bring is so much better but seldom easier. Finding the life we want involves embracing the reality of what we sign up for when we say yes to following Jesus.

Now, I understand that ideas of military, war, battles, and being a warrior are not for everyone. That's unfortunately true in the church too. However, male and female, if we are really going to be Christians, we had better be warriors. Why? As my friend John Eldredge says, "Every one of us is born into a world at war."[1] We are up against an enemy who sees all we could become, hates it, and is determined to stop it.

What We Are Up Against

In Revelation 12, we see a huge, scary, seven-headed red dragon, determined to kill Jesus when he was born. Failing at that, he turns his attention to us, Christians. Revelation also identifies him as a liar and accuser, who continues to lie to us and accuse us (v. 10). In Genesis 3:1–7, he's a subtle, deceptive, sneaky, quite convincing snake trying to cause us to question God's heart for us and to convince us that we can't trust God. In 1 Peter 5:8, he is a roaring lion seeking to devour us. In John 10:10, he is a thief seeking to steal from us. But Jesus didn't stop there; he said that the enemy also wants to kill and destroy us.

To be a successful thief, the thief must make sure the victim remains unaware of what the thief is doing as he is doing it. When was the last time you were unaware that you were being tempted to do something outside of God's plan for your life? Let me go ahead and answer. Never. We see the temptation. We don't see what a successful thief is doing as he does it. So, what is this thief that we are up against doing in our lives and stories that we are not aware of? What are we not seeing? Let that stir; we will come back to it in just a bit.

In the meantime, would our enemy be fully satisfied if we succumbed to temptation and cheated on our expense reports or clicked on something we shouldn't be watching late at night? Are you kidding me? He is after something so much deeper than that. Another Navy SEAL saying that might be helpful here is that we are "never out of the fight." What if a necessary part of redefining *Christian* is reminding ourselves of that every single day? It is a nonnegotiable on the path that leads to the life we want.

> We must not focus *only* on temptation and sin, while allowing the deeper, more insidious work of the enemy to continue to go unnoticed and unaddressed in our stories.

Please hear me. I am not minimizing my sin or yours. Our sin is a big deal. Jesus had to come to this earth, get arrested, be beaten, have the skin ripped off his back, have a crown of thorns mashed into his head and face, carry his cross up a hill, be nailed to it, and die because of our sin. It's a big, big deal, a huge deal. I'm saying we must not focus *only* on temptation and sin while allowing the deeper, more insidious work of the enemy to continue to go unnoticed and unaddressed in our stories. Jesus said, "In this world you will have trouble" (John 16:33). Not only temptation, but trouble too. The quote hanging above my desk at home accurately describes the path to the life we all want: *"Si Vis Pacem Para Bellum."* It's a Latin phrase that simply means "If you want peace, prepare for war." What if the peace we seek in this life comes not from solitude or stillness but from a daily battle that we must learn to fight? The battle is real. Yet it is rarely as obvious or in our faces as we might think.

Learning How to Fight

Five critical passages of Scripture help us see and understand the full extent of what we are up against as we follow Jesus. Let's take a quick look at each of them, starting with Ephesians 6:10–13.

> Finally, be strong in the Lord and in his mighty power. Put on the full armor of God, so that you can take your stand against the devil's schemes. For our struggle is not against flesh and blood, but against the rulers, against the authorities, against the powers of this dark world and against the spiritual forces of

evil in the heavenly realms. Therefore put on the full
armor of God, so that when the day of evil comes,
you may be able to stand your ground, and after you
have done everything, to stand.

Armor, by definition, is intended to help us defend ourselves
against an enemy's attacks, which in this context we tend to think of
as temptation to sin. So, we armor up to face our enemy. However, a
religious life of behavior management alone will never lead us to the
life that we want. Here's what I am getting to. The sin is not the win.
It's never the win. As Paul said, there is a much more elaborate scheme
playing out in each of our lives and stories. It is what the great theologian Charlie Daniels sang about in his song "The Devil Went Down
to Georgia":

> The devil went down to Georgia.
> He was lookin' for a soul to steal.
> He was in a bind 'cause he was way behind
> and he was willin' to make a deal.

We are up against an enemy that is always looking to make a
deal. In 2 Corinthians 2:11, Paul wrote, "We are not unaware of his
schemes." Paul wasn't. The question is: Are we?

When we blow it, like when I crashed and burned as a pastor more
than eighteen years ago, all the immediate focus is on what we have
done. Again, I'm not minimizing what I have done. It was terrible and
hurt the people that I love most. I still fight residual shame over it to
this very day. That part gets talked about in church. What we usually

don't talk about is how any given moment connects to the greater scheme our story's enemy is orchestrating in our life. We should. We must. The temptations we face are not random events; they are parts of a well-orchestrated, well-thought-out "scheme." The Greek word is *methodeia*. Not only does the word suggest a way of doing something deceptive, hidden, and unseen, it also implies an orderly, logical arrangement or doing something in a systematic way. From the time we are young, there is an orderly, logical, systematic attack on our hearts to keep us from seeing ourselves as God sees us.

A great example of this is the moment that Jesus had with the enemy in the wilderness at the beginning of his ministry in Luke 4. The devil tempted Jesus in three different ways, and in every single instance, Jesus fought the temptation by quoting Scripture. For so many years of my life, my takeaway from that had always been that this was Jesus demonstrating for us how we stand up against temptation. Whenever the enemy tempts you, simply quote Scripture back at him. There may be some truth to that. It can't hurt and is likely helpful, but there is so much more to this story than most of us see. It is easy to read the account of the temptation in the wilderness and fail to see the assault on Jesus' *identity*.

Go back and read the story. Two of the three temptations have this lead-in statement: "If you are the Son of God" (Luke 4:3, 9). In Luke 3, before Jesus was led into the wilderness, he was baptized, and his Father's voice was heard from heaven, saying that this was his boy, he loved him, and he was so proud of him. It was a statement of validation, of who Jesus is, of his identity. Two of the three temptations Jesus experienced were cleverly packaged in an attempt to steal that identity. Before the enemy extended the temptation, he questioned Jesus' identity. *Really, is that really who you are?* This is not a tactic specific to Jesus. We experience the same kinds of attacks every day.

The story of my crash and burn and the destruction of our family, ministry, marriage, and life has been very public now for many years. As I talk about it, I often say that Jesus and my wife, Stacy, are the real heroes in the story. I really do mean that. Stacy is a real hero of mine. She stayed with me when most would have divorced me, and God continues to do amazing things in our marriage and relationship. It is so much better today than it has ever been. I am humbled that God has blessed me with such an amazing wife and life.

Now, I need to talk about the years leading into that destructive moment. This is the rest of my story. I grew up a lower-middle-class kid in a Christian family in Louisville, Kentucky. As I mentioned before, I was redheaded, freckle faced, pale, and skinny. When people taunted me with "I would rather be dead than red on the head," I would often think, *Me too. Death would feel better than this.* Puberty came later for me than most, so in the middle school locker room, I was constantly embarrassed and trying my best to hide. I arrived in high school at 5'9" and 114 pounds. Girls were only interested in being my friend. I became very familiar with the "friend zone." At home, I was often reminded that I wasn't much to look at and that girls would never really be interested in me. I realize that this part of my pain growing up is nothing compared to many people's stories. It may be nothing compared to yours. That didn't make it any less significant.

The enemy began to tempt me at a young age, and he also began to wound me and hurt me. I've mentioned a few of my moments, my wounds. What about you? Where has the enemy come after you and caused you to question your identity, worth, and value? Take time to think about it. Nothing is out of bounds or insignificant. You may have to dig a little bit. Most of us are skilled at minimizing or distancing ourselves from these moments. The enemy is also right there trying to cover up or minimize what he has done in our lives and stories.

It's Bigger Than the Moment

Let's go back to Jesus' story. After successfully dealing with three temptations, here's what happened: "When the devil had finished all this tempting, he left him until an opportune time" (Luke 4:13).

Would the enemy have liked for Jesus to say yes to one of these temptations? Of course he would. Did he expect it? I don't think so. He left Jesus until another opportune time. These three temptations were not only aimed at getting Jesus to fail or fall in the moment by doing what the enemy asked. They were an invitation for Jesus to begin to think differently about himself. *Am I really the Son of God?* The enemy didn't argue, debate, or press into it. He didn't really want Jesus to pay much attention to it in the moment. He simply planted the seed of an idea and left it for later.

This story's point is not simply to equip us to quote Scripture to overcome temptation. God wants us to understand who we are up against and how every single day of our lives this enemy comes after our hearts. It is what Paul described in Ephesians 4:26–27: "'In your anger do not sin': Do not let the sun go down while you are still angry, and do not give the devil a foothold."

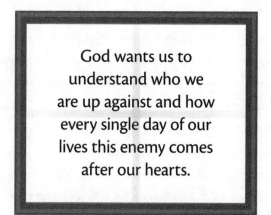

God wants us to
understand who we
are up against and how
every single day of our
lives this enemy comes
after our hearts.

Our unchecked emotions and feelings can lead not only to sin but to footholds too. This moment with Jesus shows us so much more than the fact that it is helpful for us to quote, reflect on, and lean into the Bible in times of temptations. This moment gives us a front-row seat to the strategy and schemes of our enemy. Our enemy is not only looking for us to sin; he is looking to establish footholds in our lives.

The Greek word for *foothold* is *topos*. It means a base for further advance, a place to come back to and operate from later. Too often our sole focus as Christians is on our mistakes, our sin, the things we have done. We tend to understand the sin part. Here's what we often miss. The enemy uses the things we've done against us, but he even more covertly, secretly, insidiously, and subtly uses the things that have been done to us, said to us, and said about us to establish footholds in our lives too.

So, here's a question that will change your life, a question I think we all need to learn to ask ourselves on a regular basis. *Where has the enemy established footholds in my life?* Here is what I have discovered in my own life and story. The wounds inflicted throughout the course of our lives are not random, isolated, disconnected, and unrelated. They are part of an elaborate strategy, a scheme, waged by the enemy against us. We have all been hurt in life in a variety of ways. The enemy's strategy is to connect the dots in that hurt, to build the case against us, and ultimately to keep us from seeing ourselves as God sees us.

When I was in seventh grade, the PE teacher got out the pull-up bar during gym class. Of all the guys in the class he could have called up first, you guessed it, he called me. I will never forget the humiliation of hanging there kicking and struggling to try to get above that bar just once. Nor the pain of listening to the laughter of my classmates and the teacher grow louder and louder. It felt like I hung there for hours. Then, after I had failed, he jumped up there and knocked out three or four pull-ups. You may be thinking, *No big deal. We have all been embarrassed in life.* But it took me about three decades to discover this. There is more to that moment than the immediate embarrassment and hurt. There are always messages attached to our hurt. The message that hurt delivered to me loud and clear went like this: *You are weak. You will never be strong. It's just one more reason that you will never really be a man or have what it takes, and no girl will ever really be attracted to you.* The enemy strategically connected this hurt to other hurt, to other moments of pain in my story. He connected the dots and established a foothold, a base camp, a place to work from at the next opportune time in my life and story.

So, what messages have you received? Perhaps one or more of these? *You will never really matter, never be good enough, smart enough, strong enough, beautiful enough, handsome enough, successful, worth the time of day, desired or pursued, amount to anything. You will always be second choice, a failure, a screwup, good for only one thing, good for absolutely nothing, weak, ugly, poor, stupid.*

You will always be _____.

You will never be _____.

Where has the enemy established footholds in your life? Our ability to experience the freedom that is available to us depends on our ability to answer that question. The enemy is not only trying to keep us blind to this, he also does his best to convince us when we do see it that we just need to suck it up and get over it, and that it's really not a big deal. But it's a huge deal. Paul tells us why in 2 Corinthians 10:3–5.

> For though we live in the world, we do not wage war
> as the world does. The weapons we fight with are not
> the weapons of the world. On the contrary, they have
> divine power to demolish strongholds. We demolish
> arguments and every pretension that sets itself up
> against the knowledge of God, and we take captive
> every thought to make it obedient to Christ.

The word for *stronghold* is a different Greek word than for *foothold*. The word is *ochyrōma*, which means "a strong military fortification." This is not a temporary place to advance from in the future. This is a permanent fixture, a destination, a fortress, a place of strength to fight from. If we want to fight the emptiness so many of us feel, we must understand this. Unaddressed footholds become strongholds. Both must be demolished.

As my life and story carried on, more moments piled up that seemed to affirm those negative, destructive messages about myself. A foothold was established. As the wounds continued to come, I eventually consented in agreement that those messages about me were true. That's when the enemy established a stronghold in my life. In that moment, I vowed never again to allow myself to be put in a position to demonstrate weakness. I vowed only to put myself in positions where I was sure to win. That is why, to this day, I struggle playing board games, cards, or other games that involve luck. I've healed and grown a lot, but even now, losing tries to suggest something painful to me about me.

In the end, unaddressed footholds in my life became strongholds that deeply hurt and crushed the people in this world that I love the most. We must understand that the temptations we face never come on a level or fair playing field. The enemy doesn't fight fair. It's not who he is or what he does. He never has, and he never will. Through the wounds, messages, and agreements that exist in all our stories, the playing field has been severely tilted against us. The temptations in our lives are tempting precisely because they offer medication for the pain associated with these strongholds in our lives. They offer a way to prove that the agreements upon which these strongholds are built are not true. These footholds that go unnoticed and unaddressed eventually become strongholds that must be demolished. So, how do we do that?

Awareness Is Never Enough

Sometimes the answer comes by working closely with a great therapist or counselor. I used to be ashamed to say I was seeing a counselor. There was often a certain stigma associated with that by Christians. Now, I'm jealous of people who are in a relationship with a great counselor. Trust me, it will change your life. Whether you ever decide to do that or not is up to you, but there is another way we can learn to demolish strongholds in our lives: by learning to take captive every single thought (2 Cor. 10:5). We can identify and break all the agreements we have unknowingly made with the enemy by paying attention to our thoughts, specifically the ones we have about ourselves. With every thought that enters our minds, we can learn to grab it and question it. Is this thought from God or consistent with who I understand him to be? Or could it be part of a stronghold that has already been established or that the enemy is trying to establish in my life? The best part is this: as we attempt to fight this fight, we are not alone.

Back to Luke 4, right after Jesus' temptation, he stood up in the synagogue, read from the book of Isaiah, applied it to himself, and sat down. We will talk more about this in a later chapter, but I want to note that one of the things Jesus read, one of the things that he said he came to do, is to *set our captive hearts free.*

Even if we are followers of Jesus, we are not *only* followers of Jesus. In one of my favorite movies, *We Were Soldiers*, Lieutenant Colonel Hal Moore prepared his troops for combat, saying, "We are going into battle against a tough and determined enemy." The same is true of us every day of our lives. We become prisoners to the wounds, messages, agreements, footholds, and strongholds that have been established in our lives. In my first-year Contracts class in law school, I learned that a contract does not necessarily have to be in writing to be binding. What I have since learned on my own journey through life is that it doesn't have to be in writing to be catastrophically destructive either.

The enemy cares so much less about what we do than he does about how we see ourselves because of what we've done. Long term, he can do more damage with that. If he can't take away us being with God forever, what can he do? He can continue to mess with how we believe God sees us after all we've done and all that has been done to us.

Is there any hope for this emptiness and deadness that we feel inside? Yes. His name is Jesus. He came not only to forgive us, but to help us demolish all the footholds and strongholds and to set our captive hearts free. What John Eldredge says is true: "You can't fight a battle you don't think exists."

— 4 —

Buried Treasure

*"Gaining insight into who we
are and how we became ourselves
requires some serious digging
and inspection, much the way an
archaeologist unearths the origins
and artifacts of ancient civilization
by excavating long-buried ruins."*

Reggie McNeal

Despite a few traumatizing episodes, I loved my life growing up as a lower-middle-class kid in Louisville, Kentucky, about a mile from Churchill Downs. While my mom still lives in the house I grew up in, the neighborhood is not as safe and secure as it was back then. When I was a boy, my friends and I were given the freedom to run the neighborhood. If we were given boundaries, I don't remember them now and likely disregarded them then. I do remember logging hundreds of miles on my bike. We had fun, lots of fun, building clubhouses, playing football, basketball, and baseball, riding our bikes to the local beer depot for an ice-cold bottle of Pepsi straight out of the walk-in beer cooler, cutting grass, delivering newspapers, and eventually, as we got a little older, stealing one older brother's beer.

Most of the summer was spent shirtless. Thinking back on that, I still don't quite get it. As a redhead, shocker, I didn't and don't tan well. Stacy and I went to Mexico a few years back, and I came back with sun poisoning all over my chest. It was horrible. I don't know how I pulled that off as a kid. Growing up, while I loved being outdoors and camping, I also had a special fascination with metal detectors. The idea of discovering buried treasure made my heart come alive. While I can't remember how we did it or who it belonged to, my buddies and I eventually got our hands on a metal detector. We would be disappointed when our quest for gold coins or anything of real value only turned up bottle caps, pull tabs, and other pieces of discarded, useless metal. After a few such quests, we determined that digging was a waste of time. We were unlikely to find any real treasure. That is similar to the way most of us feel about our own stories. We expect to find a whole lot more hurt, pain, guilt, and shame there than any real treasure.

A Willingness to Dig

My good buddy Morgan Snyder wrote a book called *Becoming a King*. If you are a man, especially if you are in your twenties or thirties, you really need to read that book. I wish it had been available to me thirty years ago. It would have been a game changer. Morgan unpacked the truth about the treasure that remains buried in each of our lives and stories. He said, "Failure is the doorway to deeper treasure to be discovered."[1] That resonates with me because it is my story. My greatest failure in life put me on the path to discover the deepest treasure I have discovered, the path that led to the life I had always wanted. At first glance, though, the stuff we discover may not look much like treasure. Morgan went on to say, "Much of the treasure hunt for the restoration of our souls is hidden in the story of our family of origin."[2] For many of us, not only does our family of origin *not* resemble treasure, but it is where we least desire to dig.

Having raised four daughters, Stacy and I are no strangers to Disney movies, and one of my all-time favorites is *The Lion King*. One of my favorite scenes is when Rafiki, the mandrill who serves as shaman to the Pride Lands, hits young Simba with his walking stick out of the blue. When Simba asks why he did that, Rafiki says, "What does it matter? It's in the past." Simba responds, "Yeah, but it still hurt!" Rafiki's reply is priceless: "Ah, yes, the past can hurt. But the way I see it, you can either run from it or learn from it. Now what are you going to do?" Most of us have done our best to bury and forget the painful experiences in our past. We have chosen to run from it rather than learn from it. We can't imagine that it could hold treasure.

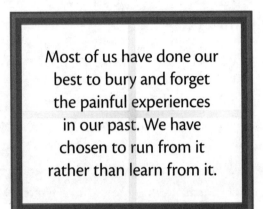

Most of us have done our best to bury and forget the painful experiences in our past. We have chosen to run from it rather than learn from it.

My initial meeting with my counselor Rob, over eighteen years ago now, did not get us off to a fantastic start. I really liked Rob and could tell that, despite the brutal facts and circumstances that landed me in his office, he had nothing but compassion for me and kindness toward me. I was convinced that he really did care and genuinely desired to help me. Having said that, when I discovered the journey he intended to lead me on, I was flat-out pissed. Here I was, my marriage hanging by a thread, my wife and daughters heartbroken and crushed because of what I had done. I was sleeping on the couch, wondering when I would be asked to leave and feeling pretty convinced our marriage wouldn't make it. I was like, *Dude, I need your help with that. I need your help with my marriage, not my mommy stuff.* Despite my objections, Rob remained firm and kind. One of my first assignments was to write down every hurtful moment I could remember, going back into my childhood as far as I could remember. Initially, I didn't take him seriously. I thought, *You know what? I don't think I am going to do that.* But I quickly realized that if there was any hope for our marriage, our family, Stacy's and my daughters' hearts, it would come through cooperating with Rob.

As I began to compile the list, it was difficult to write in my journal some of the things that surfaced. It seemed a bit ridiculous. That moment wasn't as bad as some I have heard from others, though. *Yes, that happened, but who cares, it really wasn't a big deal.* If it felt that way to me—and it did—it shouldn't have. I struggled at first to compile the list. As a man, I had been conditioned to get up, rub some dirt on it, and say it didn't really hurt. That conditioning—and comparing my moments to others'—almost kept me from writing anything down. Then, I remembered Rob's words: "It doesn't matter whether you think it should have hurt or how minimal you believe it to be; just write it down. Put it on the list." Reluctantly I did just that. When I was done, I had listed thirty-five moments of pain, going back to when I was about six. Most of them felt small and insignificant. I was embarrassed to admit that some of them had hurt me at all.

Over the next three years, Rob helped me understand the connection between all those moments. I began to see the messages associated with them, the themes that had developed, the conclusions I had reached, and the agreements I had made about me. For the first time in my life, I realized that, unintentionally, I had been trying to arrange my life to avoid feeling that way ever again. I had been running from my past, but now, it was time for me to learn from it. There was much buried treasure to be discovered. I didn't know this path would lead me to the life I had always been looking for. It was to be a long, hard journey, and my life would never be the same.

Back to the Future

I soon discovered that the rest of my story (my future) would be determined by the healing I experienced in the rest of my story (my past). The ultimate treasure was discovering the answers to how and why I had blown up my life. I had refused to accept the answers that Christians projected on me (being a porn or sex addict), but I hadn't found the true answer on my own. The treasure hunt that Rob facilitated didn't offer justification for what I did. But it helped me *understand* it and do the work necessary to ensure there wouldn't be a next time. With Rob's encouragement and support, I wanted to deal with, once and for all, whatever had led me down this brutal path. The hunt required digging into my story.

So often, we reduce the Christian life to having our own Jesus "salvation" experience, and then getting busy living for Jesus while trying to forget all about our past. Going back to the diagram in chapter 1, this is two-circle living. That is what the eighty or so people were doing who were a part of Discovery Church when I first arrived. They didn't know any other way. Focusing on the rest of your story is a radical shift away from that. What does it look like for you to begin to dig, to excavate, to uncover the stuff in your story and then invite Jesus into the mess and experience him in that? What if you were to uncover and bring to Jesus not just the bad things you have done but also all the things that have been done to, said to, and said about you? What about all of the experiences you didn't want, ask for, or cause that still shape you? What would it look like for you to experience Jesus in all of that? All these questions point to the second leg of our journey in part 2.

So many of us have experienced Jesus' forgiveness of sin. Yet, many of us have not experienced Jesus in the depths and details of our own stories and all the healing, redemption, restoration, and absolute free-dom that come from that. It is a part of the incredible rescue Jesus wants to accomplish in each of our lives and stories. By missing out on ourselves, we also cause the people closest to us to miss out too. Brennan Manning said it this way: "In a futile attempt to erase our past, we deprive the community of our healing gift. If we conceal our wounds, out of fear and shame, our inner darkness can neither be illu-minated nor become a light for others."[3] Not only can you experience deep healing in your own story, others can benefit from your story too. Your story is not just for you. Once you become a follower of Jesus, you have been and continue to be rescued by Jesus so you can help rescue others. We will talk about that more in the final part of the book.

> Your story is not just for you. Once you become a follower of Jesus, you have been and continue to be rescued by Jesus so you can help rescue others.

For now, there's buried treasure to be discovered in all our stories. Start digging, and then keep digging. I attended my very first Wild at Heart Boot Camp in February of 2008. Since then, I have attended four more, an Advanced Camp, a Become Good Soil Retreat, and a

Crucible Project Retreat. I will continue to. Why? Because there is always more digging to do, more to discover, more healing to experience on this journey with Jesus.

Having said that, let's spend a minute talking practically about how we begin to dig for this buried treasure in our lives. The best part of what I am getting ready to tell you is: this stuff will help you whether or not you are a Christian. Here are six steps to move you closer to the life that you want.

1. Think as far back in your life and story as you can remember about times and moments that hurt you, then write them down.

2. Don't minimize or compare—just write them down.

3. Don't try to figure out why something hurt—just admit that it did.

4. Consider what message that moment spoke to you about you. Often, what happened in the moment is less painful than the message you received from that moment.

5. As you consider these moments, think about whether any other moments have suggested something similar to you about you. Are there themes that have been established or conclusions that you have reached about yourself in your life and story? Sometimes a moment doesn't point to anything new. It simply reinforces something you

already believe to be true that you don't want to be
true about you.

6. Never stop digging. We must recognize that this
process is not one and done. Some of this stuff is
buried deep. We have to stay committed to digging.

What started as a list of about thirty-five moments has grown to
over eighty in the past eighteen years of my life. If you want real life
change, you have to discover your story *and* stay in it. I hope that you
will dig. It changed my life forever, and it will yours too.

Story Reveals Glory

There is one more thing we haven't talked about that you will discover
as you begin to dig. As you dig, you will discover the deep desires of
your heart, the things that make your heart come alive. Let me give
you an example. When I began my own excavation journey, along with
the pain leading to my wounding and brokenness, I discovered a lot of
good memories involving camping trips, trail maps, caves, mountains,
my dad's stories from WWII and Patton's Third Army, my love for
the military, the United States Marine Corps, fire, knives, guns, and
sports. I encourage you to keep your eyes peeled for two important,
distinct types of moments—those that hurt you and those that made
your heart jump or come alive. See, something else has been buried
in our lives—our glory, our deep desires, all that we have each been
uniquely created by God to be. Before we leave this, we must spend a
little time talking about the treasure to be discovered in that.

My dad grew up in the "sticks" of Kentucky, down in the south-central part of the state. After being drafted out of high school for WWII, he returned to his small hometown to finish high school. After graduating, he moved to the big city of Louisville, Kentucky, where he took a job with an aluminum company that later became Atlantic Richfield. He stayed there almost forty years.

After my sophomore year of high school, I found myself looking for a summer job. A friend and mentor, Terry, from the small church we attended, persuaded me to come work for him and his father, who owned two jewelry stores in town. The money was less than jobs in the fast-food world, but they promised to teach me to repair watches and jewelry. I ended up discovering that I was gifted at working with my hands, and I enjoyed the work. Two years later, upon graduation from high school, they offered me a full-time position making a whopping $10,500 per year. (It was 1982.) That was all I needed to hear. My girl-friend at the time, Stacy, had decided to stay home for college. I loved her and wanted to marry her, and this would provide me the opportunity to do just that. So, Stacy started college classes immediately upon graduation from high school, and I took a job as a watchmaker and began to try to save money for our desired future together.

That was the path and trajectory we were on until one day when Stacy told me about an encounter between college classes. Walking through the old student center at the University of Louisville, she saw a Marine recruiting college students for Officer Candidates School (OCS). Now, I absolutely love the United States Marine Corps. That has been true since I was a boy. My dad was not the veteran who remained quiet about what he had seen and experienced in the war. He told me stories all the time. I wanted to know the stories behind his jacked-up, gnarly feet, which had suffered severe frostbite in shallow foxholes in France during the war. "Do you know what I was doing forty years ago today?" was a common conversation starter for us. More than once, my dad told me, "Son, those damn Marines were so stinkin' tough." I honestly probably never heard a word he said after that. It was all I needed to hear. If I wanted to be tough, there was only one response. I had to be a Marine.

That desire had been long buried in me until the day Stacy brought me the information she had picked up for me after talking to the Marine officer selection officer. I had all but given up on that dream. I was doing what I could to make life work and preparing for our upcoming wedding. I had no idea about OCS and what being a Marine officer was all about. But the material Stacy brought me reignited my long-dormant desire. So, I called the number on the brochure and set up a meeting with Captain Breen, the officer selection officer whose office was down on the edge of campus. When we met, he indicated that to pursue this, I had to be a college student. Stacy and I talked. We decided that I would cut back to part-time work and become a full-time student so I could pursue this deep desire in my heart.

I will never forget the moment I told my dad what I was planning to do. We were standing in front of the window in the dining room near the back door. More than the spot, I will never forget what my dad said to me. I knew he loved me, was for me, and wanted to see me succeed. When he heard what I was planning to do, he said, "Son, why in the world would you do something like that? You need to stay the course." It was all that he himself had ever known. Find a trade, stay with the trade, don't rock the boat, provide for your family. As much as I wanted to please my dad, I refused to do it. I started to chase the deep

desire of my heart and attended United States Marine Corps Officer
Candidate School the following summer.

Desire Leads to Destiny

We all have moments in our lives and stories when events, circumstances, and well-meaning people suggest that the deep desires of our
hearts really don't matter. This is especially true in the church world.
If your experience with church has been anything like mine, you've
received the message that it is all about what God wants for your life.
Your desires don't matter. In fact, acting on your desires will only get
you into trouble. The accepted "Christian" course is that you must kill
the desires of your evil heart. While some desires (temptations) may
need to be killed, a big part of finding the path to the life that we want
is understanding how we have mishandled the desires of our hearts.

The enemy in your story knows that, if desire is unleashed in your
life, it will lead you directly to God and the life that he has for you.
Desire is the map that carries us back to our place in the story. If the
enemy can't trap it, he will try to kill it, get you to bury your heart, to
live a life of religious duty. Is that what the "Christian" life has been
reduced to for you? If so, hang on. There's hope. There's more, so much
more. The invitation of Jesus is for us to be people of passion who live
out of the desires of our hearts.

One of the best books I have read on desire is a book that was
originally called *The Journey of Desire* by John Eldredge. I would challenge you to read it. It changed my life and my approach to life forever.
John did a phenomenal job of unpacking desire in so much more depth
than I could possibly accomplish here, so I want to leave you with one

simple quote: "Desire reveals design, and design reveals destiny."[4] Desire ultimately leads to destiny. So, before we leave this "discover your story" piece, here is one last, very important question. What have you done with the deep desires of your heart?

The enemy in your story clearly sees your glory, the essence of all that you have been uniquely created by God to be. Do you know who often doesn't see it, who most struggles to see it? You. Ultimately, a big part of being rescued by Jesus is restoring our ability to see ourselves as he sees us. It is a big part of what he is after and what too few have experienced.

Glory is an interesting thing. What the enemy and others see clearly in us, we struggle to see in ourselves. It remains buried treasure for us. This is why we so desperately need a few of the right people in our lives to do this journey with. They can see and speak into our glory, which is so necessary and such a source of encouragement to us. "I see in you" are, have been, and will always be four of the most powerful words on the planet. We will talk about that thoroughly in chapter 10.

We have no problem seeing each other's glory. It is right in front of us. It is where jealousy and envy get stirred up in us. There is no assault by the enemy on our ability to see someone else's glory. The enemy's assault is on my ability to look in the mirror and see mine. It points to the significance of relationship, two is better than one, us needing each other. It points to the need for each of us to dig for it in our own lives and stories too. Our deep desires are a part of the gold to be discovered as we dig into our own stories. The path to your glory is always back into and through your story.

Reggie McNeal said, "Self awareness touches all of the other disciplines because it is foundational to every other element of greatness."[5]

It is foundational to the life that every single one of us is looking for too. Mickey Mantle is quoted as saying, "It's unbelievable how much you don't know about the game you've been playing all your life." I have found and continue to find that to be true of the Christian life.

Excavating your story is an unavoidable part of the path that leads to the life that you want, the life that you have been searching for your entire Christian life. Much buried treasure yet to be discovered is there. You can continue to run from it, or you can begin to learn from it. The choice is yours. Rafiki's question for Simba is my question today for you: "So, what are you going to do?" You can live a purpose-driven life and never really find or experience all the life that Jesus came to bring you. I don't know about you, but I want all of it. However, discovery and awareness are not enough. So, what do we do with the buried treasure we discover? Let's keep going. There is so much to talk about on this path that leads to the life we want.

Part Two

Experience Jesus

— 5 —

Why Church and Religion Don't Work

"Some want to live within the sound of church or chapel bell; I want to run a rescue shop, within a yard of hell."

C. T. Studd

You may be familiar with the television show *M*A*S*H*. The acronym in the title stands for "mobile army surgical hospital," and the series was about Mobile Army Hospital Unit 4077, made up of surgeons, nurses, medics, and other support personnel during the Korean War. The big idea behind a MASH unit was to get help closer to the front lines so that the wounded could be treated sooner and with greater success. It makes sense. If you are in a war, you had better have a MASH unit for the wounded, fallen, and dying. So, what does that have to do with this book?

We sometimes face issues around our health, marriage, finances, relationships, work, and life in general that cause us to feel heavy. They often leave us broken, hurting, wounded, messed up, confused, doubting, hopeless, and uncertain. Even when things are good, we know that challenges will come again in the future. I'm not trying to be negative, it's just the way life works. Life is messy. A person wounded in war ends up in a MASH unit. But what about us? Where do we go with our stuff? Church? Really, how helpful has that been? Has that been your experience? Have you, like me, ever felt like your life, story, and/ or current circumstances were just a little too messy for the church? It is not uncommon.

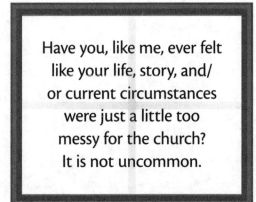

Have you, like me, ever felt like your life, story, and/ or current circumstances were just a little too messy for the church? It is not uncommon.

Should our stories ever be too messy for the church? There's a story in Mark 1 that sheds some light on that question.

A man with leprosy came to him and begged him on his knees, "If you are willing, you can make me clean."

Jesus was indignant. He reached out his hand and touched the man. "I am willing," he said. "Be clean!" Immediately the leprosy left him and he was cleansed. (vv. 40–42)

Jesus, who had been traveling around preaching, casting out demons, and healing a bunch of people, was approached by a man with leprosy. Leprosy was an incredibly progressive, destructive, and contagious disease. If you thought you had it, the priest would examine you, quarantine you for a few weeks, and then declare you "clean" or "unclean." Leviticus 13 said that the unclean must live away from everyone else and cry out "Unclean!" if anyone came near. It sounds cruel, but the isolation was necessary so that the whole community would not be infected.

Keeping lepers away from people is logical. It makes sense. Keeping lepers out of church is also logical. However, it can lead to a way of thinking that sometimes we need to exclude certain people. So, having been excluded by the "church," this man approached Jesus. The Bible says Jesus was indignant. But Jesus was not angry with this man. He wasn't saying, "Don't get that stuff near me." Jesus got angry when people were isolated, alone, hopeless, excluded, or led to believe that they were beyond his grace, mercy, forgiveness, and healing. As you know, I've been there in my own life and story. There is nothing worse than feeling like an outcast. We don't know why Jesus was indignant, but we do know that one is never beyond his reach or excluded from his touch.

Moving toward the Mess

Having completed undergrad and law school at the University of Louisville, I am a huge University of Louisville Cardinals fan. In 2013, our men's basketball team won the national championship. I will never forget picking up my teenage daughter in the family room, spinning her around, and jumping up and down. I don't think she will forget that either. She's extremely happy to this day that none of her friends were there to see it. We hadn't won it all since 1986, when I was a student there. I was pumped. Despite my joy, that 2013 national championship was later vacated by the NCAA and given to the team we beat in the championship game, the University of Michigan. There were allegations of using strippers to recruit student athletes, and apparently the NCAA is not good with that. Rightfully so. As much as I hate to acknowledge it, the championship banner now hangs in the Crisler Center in Ann Arbor, Michigan.

Although I enjoyed winning the championship game, that game was not my favorite moment in the tournament. In the first half of the game we played against Duke to advance to the Final Four, one of our guards, Kevin Ware, jumped, came down funny, and snapped the lower half of his right leg below the knee in half. About six inches of bone protruded through the skin. Even if you are not a basketball or March Madness fan, you might remember that moment. People panicked. It was the most gruesome injury many of us may ever see. Players cried, gasped, looked away, and fell to the floor. One player even threw up in a towel. And then there was Luke Hancock. He immediately went to his teammate lying there with this gross, distorted leg, and as the medical staff cared for him, he grabbed his hand, patted his chest, and prayed for him. In that moment, when most wouldn't or couldn't get close, he was right there with his friend. It was like Jesus with the leper all over again.

This is who Jesus is and what experiencing Jesus is all about. There was nothing in the leper's life Jesus was unwilling to touch. There was nothing he had done or that had been done to him that made Jesus uncomfortable with him. Unfortunately, that is often the difference between Jesus and the church. Please hear me. I love the church. I have not given up on the church. I can't and won't. Jesus said that he is going to build it and that hell is not going to stop it, and I believe him. I think that the church can be great. When it lines up with what Jesus intended for it to be, it can be the hope of the world. But church is not the destination. It was never intended to be. Ultimately, all of us need what this man needed: to get to Jesus.

Our Preference Problem

You can read the rest of the story in Mark 1. After healing the leper, Jesus told him to show himself to the priest. Instead, he walked away telling others about what Jesus did for him. I think this man's decision points to one of the biggest tragedies and challenges facing Christians, the church, and the cause of Jesus today. There was no reason for this man not to go to the priest. He was no longer unclean. He would no longer be excluded, and it was what Jesus told him to do. But he didn't. Why? Maybe he was selfish, and all he cared about was his own most pressing issue. But couldn't it also be he didn't care about being welcomed now that he was cleaned up and better, because he couldn't get over how he had been treated when he wasn't? It wouldn't be surprising if he wanted nothing to do with those people.

This thing we do called church should be a MASH unit. The problem is that we prefer to be a hospital. Hospitals have a thorough admissions process. Hospitals ask you questions, make you fill out a bunch of forms, check and verify your insurance, and then have you wait over there while they see if they can accept you and help you. You can't just walk in and expect to stay. Hospitals are clean, sterile environments, not messy at all, and have the proper safeguards in place. Some even prefer to take it one step further. Maybe the church can be an immediate care center, a place where it is so much easier to say, "You know what, we can't handle your kind of problem or mess here. Sorry." No, the church should be a MASH unit. Life is messy, and if church is real, authentic, genuine, vulnerable, and true—all the words we are so quick to drop on our websites—then church will be messy too. Too often, it's not. We don't allow it to be.

I always loved the opening credits on *M*A*S*H*—especially that moment when the choppers and trucks came in, full of the wounded and dying, and every single person in the entire camp had one focus and mission: rescue. Everyone dropped what they were doing and ran as hard as they could toward those wounded and dying people, toward the mess. They were hyper-focused on getting people inside, stopping the bleeding, and getting people the help they needed as quickly as possible.

Let's think through that from a church context. Not getting the people in so they can read through the Bible in a year. Not getting them in so they can learn to pray more and better. Not getting them in so they can memorize Scripture. Not getting them in so they will give, serve, tithe, curse less, and switch to light beer (or drink beer in secret like all good Christians do). There is one mission: getting as many people as possible inside so they can experience not us, but Jesus.

The Exact Same Chain

But instead, here we are in the church, two thousand years later, and "leprosy" is still an epidemic around the church. We are still creating "leper colonies." We don't call them lepers, but adulterers, gay people, drug addicts, bisexuals, transgender people, porn addicts, sex addicts, divorced people, queer people, alcoholics, separated people, remarried people, people who have had abortions, unclean, unclean, unclean. You get the point. Here we are two thousand years later, and the church still thinks it is up to us to decide who is clean and unclean. How about this? We are all lepers. Apart from Jesus, none of us are anything. The Bible makes it clear that we have all blown it and fallen short (Rom. 3:23). If we were all hanging on to a chain over a deep canyon, how many links of that chain would have to break for us to fall? Just one. Guess what, it wouldn't matter which link it was. We have to get that—not "You've done what? Oh, I would never do that!" but instead "You've broken the chain? Yeah, me too, come on in." How would our world change if the church were more like this?

Part of the challenge is that we all choose our priorities that determine how we live our lives. We all have hot-button topics and issues that are important to us and other issues that fall way down the list. We bring that thinking into the church too. For some it is about the music, fog machines, lights, how we dress, whether we take communion every week, or whether we baptize by sprinkling or dunking people. We all have a hierarchy, an order of importance.

My buddy Jim Burgen is the pastor of Flatirons Church near Boulder, Colorado, one of the biggest churches in the country. He said he once got an email that read something like this: "We are new to your church, and we like what we see, but could you please tell us where you stand on gay marriage, abortion, and Israel?" Jim said, "It's funny. I never get any emails wanting to know our position on self-righteousness, pride, greed, or hypocrisy." We all have our priorities.

We have a way of ordering sin too. There are sins, and then there are "really bad sins," like adultery, murder, abortion, and homosexuality. I don't know what sins make your top-five list, but most of us have one. The sin in my past makes the top five on nearly _every_ Christian's list. I have felt and experienced that, and I can tell you, it's not fun, especially if you plan on continuing to hang out with Christians.

If that is your story, I'm sorry. Me too. I have been written off, told that I was outside the grace of God, and had people I thought were friends walk away and refuse to talk to me ever again. I have been on the receiving end of all this, and yet, guess what? There is still a tendency within me to do it to others. I'm not proud of it, and I am working on it, but it's still true.

There's No Order

About ten years ago, our DCC (Discovery Church Colorado) men were at a camp in the mountains of Colorado for our annual retreat. During the last couple of days, we shared the dining facility with a small group of women from another church. When I went down to get coffee on Saturday morning, a few ladies were talking about "Pastor Ted" and how great he was. As I walked down the hall, I realized they were talking about Pastor Ted Haggard, who had crashed and burned while leading a church in Colorado Springs the year after I had crashed in North Carolina. He was much more well-known, which had made his crash much more public and his fall probably harder than mine. I can't help but have some compassion.

Continuing down the hall, I saw Ted's wife, Gayle, writing notes and getting ready to lead and teach that small group of women. I had always wanted to meet her, so I walked into the room and introduced myself. I told her I really admired and respected her for standing by and with Ted in the storm. I said that I had a beautiful wife who also stood by me when I really screwed up, broke her heart, and crushed our family, and that I really respected her for doing the same. I remember thinking, as I walked away from that conversation, that I should have made it clear to her that I didn't do what Ted did. My sin was different. I almost turned around at that moment to go clarify that. How jacked up is that? Definitely not my best moment.

There I was, prioritizing sin, putting things in order, from bad to worse. Where does that come from? Is prioritizing sin about being holy and righteous, or is it just another way to help me feel better about myself? Could it be medicating unresolved pain and hurt in my own story? We have to ask the question.

Another example of our tendency to prioritize can be found in Mark 12. A religious leader who wanted to prioritize the commandments asked Jesus which of the commandments was most important. Jesus didn't pick one of the top ten. Former *Late Show* host David Letterman once had his top ten every night, and God has his too. They made a movie about it, *The Ten Commandments*. Of the 613 commandments in the Old Testament, God only wrote ten of them on stone tablets. But Jesus didn't go there. Jesus chose two that were not even written together in Scripture. One of them is recorded a chapter after the ten commandments are relisted in Deuteronomy 5. The other is number seventeen in a list of about thirty-five dos and don'ts in Leviticus 19. So, with 613 choices and a well-established top-ten list, Jesus said, "Here are my top two. Love God, and love people."

They say that people who live in glass houses shouldn't throw stones, and here I was, a guy with a jacked-up story who cheated on his wife; who has a list of sins in his life a mile long; in heavy need of grace, mercy, forgiveness, and love; walking away from a conversation with Gayle Haggard and *judging* her husband, Ted. God says love God, love people, but it's a whole lot easier to love God and judge people, isn't it? The Pharisees were notorious for it, and we Christians have a bit of a reputation for it too. Something has got to change. Here's something to think about. Is our tendency to judge others really about their sin, or is it more about our struggle to love ourselves?

When I was a pastor in North Carolina, before I blew up my life and stepped away from ministry, I loved people. I really did. I wanted every person I met to know and love Jesus. I was passionate about it. But if I am honest, I loved people to be loved back. There were strings attached. It took a lot of counseling for me to realize it, but it was true. I loved people, but my ability to love was limited by my ability to love myself.

Jesus said, "Love your neighbor as yourself" (Mark 12:31). Can I just say this? I have learned this the hard way. We don't have the capacity to truly love people until we allow Jesus to rescue us and help us to love ourselves. "As yourself" implies that self-love is in place before we begin to love others. If this idea of loving yourself seems contrary to what you grew up learning in church, I get that. Me too. I missed it too. "Deny yourself" gets a lot more attention and seems a lot more holy. But "love yourself" is foundational. It's hard to deny yourself when you're hyper-focused on finding a way to medicate your pain and feel better about you. How much of our tendency to judge others is really about how we feel about ourselves?

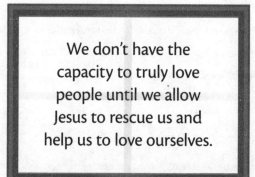

We don't have the capacity to truly love people until we allow Jesus to rescue us and help us to love ourselves.

If you have been around church, you know what Jesus said about loving God and loving people. The challenge is in living it. Listen to what Paul said about love in Romans 13:8–9:

> Let no debt remain outstanding, except the continu-
> ing debt to love one another, for whoever loves others
> has fulfilled the law. The commandments, "You shall
> not commit adultery," "You shall not murder," "You
> shall not steal," "You shall not covet," and whatever

other command there may be, are summed up in this
one command: "Love your neighbor as yourself."

All the commandments we are writing down, memorizing, sum-
marizing, prioritizing, putting in order, teaching, and using to judge
others are all summed up in one command. Love your neighbor as
yourself. Jesus made it clear in John 13:35: "By this everyone will know
that you are my disciples, if you" take communion, dress nice, don't
drink, don't curse, don't smoke, quote the Bible, pray in public, go to
church. No! None of that. I'm not saying those things are not important. I'm just saying that, according to Jesus, that is not how anyone
will know that we line up with him. They will know by the love we
have for all people in the world around us.

It's All about Love

Somewhere along the way, we have lost that. Somehow, somewhere
along the way, the style and volume of our music have become more
important than loving people. How we dress, whether we take communion every week, not drinking or cursing, how we vote, a bunch
of stuff that the Bible is not even clear on or doesn't even really
address—these things have become more important to us than loving
people. Life is too short. People are dying every day without hope. We
must stop majoring on minors in the church. To paraphrase the great
theologian Jon Bon Jovi, somehow, someway, we Christians must stop
giving love a bad name.

A MASH unit doesn't look like much—a bunch of tents and
wooden structures with no statues, fountains, stained glass, flower

gardens, or gift shops. But statistics have proven that wounded or dying soldiers have a 97 percent chance of surviving if they can get to a MASH unit. This should be true of the church. How many people could and would experience Jesus if you and I were willing to roll up our sleeves and begin to make this reality, one person at a time?

— 6 —

Something to Prove

*"I love it when people doubt me. It makes
me work harder to prove them wrong."*

Derek Jeter

———◇———

I arrived in Colorado Springs in August 2008 so excited. I had been
out of ministry for three years since my crash, had benefited greatly
from weekly counseling with Rob, and was so grateful that God was
willing to restore me and give me another chance. A lot of pastors and
Christians did not seem to be for it, but it was obvious to both Stacy
and me that God was in it. About six months after we arrived in the
Springs, I met with another pastor in town who also had grown up in
Kentucky. From the moment I walked into his office, I knew he had
a major character flaw—he was a University of Kentucky fan. Despite

that glaring deficiency, we had a good conversation. He welcomed me to town and asked about my story. I told him the good, the bad, and the ugly, including my moral failure as a pastor in my first ministry. Surprisingly, he didn't flinch. Instead, he invited me to tell my story to a group of local pastors at an annual overnight retreat at the Navigators' Glen Eyrie Retreat Center on the west side of town. I accepted and looked forward to the opportunity.

A few months later, I found myself in the Glen Eyrie Castle with about forty or so other local pastors. The pastor who had invited me welcomed everyone and introduced me. Within a few minutes, I realized I had made a huge mistake. As I began to describe my crash and burn, the room started to feel like a scene in the movie *Frozen*. It was obvious the crowd was not comfortable with my story. Unfortunately, though, there was no turning back. I finished telling my story, thanked them for having me, and went back to my seat. The remaining twenty-four hours of the retreat were uncomfortable for me. Only a handful of pastors talked with me. I felt guilt and shame rising in me again. By extension, I felt unwelcome and unwanted in the city, like there was no place for me or any church I might lead. I felt like the disqualified, damaged goods that other pastors I had known had made me out to be. How did I respond? I'm not proud of this, but in my mind, I flipped every one of them off—yes, double one-finger salutes—and walked away thinking, *I don't want you in my life. I don't need you in my life. We will never be friends.* I put my head down, more determined than ever to do what God had brought me to Colorado Springs to do. A recurring three-word theme emerged in my life and story: "I'll show you." I was once again an invalidated man with something to prove. The ironic thing is that some of the guys in that room are now some of my very closest friends. We will talk more about that near the end of the book. Yes, I will do anything to keep you reading.

A Common Theme

Having something to prove was nothing new for me. It had been a recurring theme throughout the course of my life. My guess is that, just like Derek Jeter's quote at the beginning of this chapter, it exists in some form in most of our lives and stories. People doubt us, and we work harder to prove them wrong. Looking back, I realize how that moment fifteen years ago at Glen Eyrie connected with other, similar moments in my story.

While I didn't think about it at the time, the response of those pastors felt familiar. It was like others I had experienced in the previous three years of my life. It also connected with many moments in my story going back much further than that. An elder in the church I grew up in knew of other mistakes in my past and thought I should not be a deacon, much less a pastor. He had opposed me and tried to limit my ministry opportunities for years—and for a long time, I had been determined to prove him wrong. Another pastor, after I blew up my first ministry, contacted the elders in churches that were talking to me, trying to sabotage my chances of ever being a pastor again. God bless both of their little hearts! They are both good men who love Jesus and have done great things for the kingdom—good men who I was determined to prove wrong. That moment at Glen Eyrie felt very familiar to me. They could think what they wanted, but I walked away from them more determined than ever. I was going to do everything in my power to prove every single one of them wrong.

Earlier I told the story of my seventh-grade gym teacher who humiliated me on the pull-up bar. About eight years later, I graduated from a summer of OCS in the Marine Corps. If you aren't aware, pull-ups are a significant thing in the Marine Corps. In fact, they are one of the three parts of the PFT (physical fitness test). By that time, I had built up my upper-body strength to do a significant number of pull-ups. A few months after graduation, I was back home and attending an event at my old high school. Guess who was there? My seventh-grade gym teacher, then in his mid-sixties. I couldn't get to him fast enough. He said, "Hey, Greg, how are you?" I said, "Great. Are you ready to do some pull-ups?"

He looked at me like I had two heads. I can't blame him. It's a weird way to start a conversation with someone you haven't seen in years. I couldn't help it. He had humiliated me in front of my class-mates, confirming the message that I was weak and would never be strong. I realize now how jacked up that was. I needed to prove him wrong. I had to prove him wrong. Again, I felt like I had something to prove. Have you seen this "something to prove" tendency in your own life and story? You, my friend, are not alone.

In 2014, when Stacy and I were heading out for a thirty-year anniversary trip to the Dominican Republic, I was looking to download two or three books on my Kindle for the trip. As I was browsing through Special Operations books, a title caught my attention: *The Trident*. A trident is an insignia earned and worn by Navy SEALs, but it was the subtitle of the book that grabbed me: *The Forging and Reforging of a Navy SEAL Leader*. I remember thinking, *What happened that he had to be reforged? Did he mess up, make a mistake, blow things up? What's his story?* I could not wait to read the book, and it did not disappoint.

The Trident is the story of Navy SEAL Jason Redman. Jason was an enlisted Navy SEAL for several years before attending and graduating from Old Dominion University and becoming a Navy SEAL Officer. In 2005 in Afghanistan, he was leading his team on a mission and made a foolish decision that could have cost his entire team their lives. Fortunately, they all survived, but Jason thought his career as a Navy SEAL might be cut short. Here's more of Jason's story from his own perspective:

> When I was younger, if you told me I couldn't do something, I'd use your words as fuel to prove you wrong. Call it a blessing, or a curse. It has been both throughout my life. Believe me, I've heard it all before. Jay, you're too small, too skinny, too unfocused, too reckless, too cocky, too wild. Not good enough, not smart enough, a loose cannon, a "social hand grenade." Yeah, keep talking. You're just feeding the inferno.[1]

Like many of our stories, Jason's contained a lot of unresolved stuff, which he carried with him into his role as a Navy SEAL. He was carrying it with him on that mission in Afghanistan. Here's how he described it: "Unfortunately, the desire to prove myself was in danger of blinding me to my duty to lead. Good combat leaders not only know when to fight, they know when not to fight."[2] Jason's need to prove himself almost cost him and several of his team their lives. Again, one of the most dangerous things in this world is an invalidated person with something to prove. We will come back to Jason's story later in more detail. It continues to be a source of inspiration to many and is especially relevant to those of us who see and recognize this "something to prove" thing living in us.

Who You Are and Are Becoming

My first meeting with Craig McConnell of the Wild at Heart team was in the fall of 2008. That meeting launched me into an eight-year friendship and a mentorship journey that changed my life. I will talk more about all that Craig's friendship did for me in the chapters to come. For now, I want to mention how Craig saw and helped me address my "something to prove" issue. I have always been an intense, driven, take-the-hill kind of guy. Craig would often speak to that: "Hey, Greg, you know this striving, driving, relentless, take-the-hill thing you have going on?" The first few times he went there, it fired me up. Something inside me swelled with anticipation, waiting for him to praise the unique wiring and gifting God had given me. Then he would say, "Yeah, God's not in that."

At first, it surprised me. If I am honest, it flat-out pissed me off. Over the course of the next eight years, we continually revisited that place and space in my life. The "something to prove" drive does not die quickly or easily. As I write this, I am looking up at a plaque on the wall in my home office. It is a picture of me and Craig with a quote that I don't believe was original to him but one he would continually say to me: "Who you are and are becoming is more important than anything that you will ever do." In other words, "Greg, you don't have anything to prove." It took some time for me to believe that.

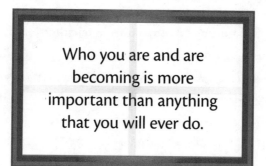

Who you are and are becoming is more important than anything that you will ever do.

In the early days of our journey together, I was often whining to Craig about how our church seemed to be stuck. One day, when I walked into his office, he quickly identified that I was off and that we needed to pray. He asked God to speak, and we sat in silence for about ten minutes (it seemed like sixty) and just listened. Then, Craig asked me what I got, what God said to me. I was not accustomed to this type of listening prayer, and my mind had raced everywhere during the silence, so I threw the question back to him: "What did *you* get?" He said, "God took me to a scene in the movie *Gladiator*." It is the scene where the evil Emperor Commodus asks Maximus to take off his helmet and tell him his name. Maximus says "My name is Gladiator" and turns away. Commodus demands that he take off his helmet and say his name. Maximus turns and takes off his helmet. This time his response is not "Gladiator." I'm not going to recite his speech here, but here's the gist: "This is who I am, and this is what I am going to do."

Craig said, "Greg, the Father is saying that to you. This is who you are, who he has created you to be. You have nothing to prove. Now be bold, and go and do what he is asking you to do." That moment was a turning point not only in our church but also in my own journey to overcome this deep-seated message I had lived by for years that I had something to prove. Two days after Craig lost his battle with leukemia in August 2016, I had a gladiator helmet with Craig's initials and the words "Rescued to Rescue" in Hebrew tattooed on the inside of my right forearm. It's a reminder of who I am and have been created by God to be, a reminder every day that I have nothing to prove.

My journey with Craig helped me understand the big difference in living *forgiven* and living *free*. The only way to live free is to experience more of Jesus, to continue to experience all that Jesus came to do for me. The path to freedom required me to break the agreements I had made over the course of my life. One of the biggest agreements was that I would never measure up and would always have something to prove. Craig and I spent a lot of time breaking agreements together. I had to refuse to be defined by what I had done. It was what I had done; it was not who I was. I needed to experience more than forgiveness from Jesus. I needed his healing, redemption, and restoration, his help dealing with all the guilt, shame, disqualification, and diminishment. Jesus came into that place and space with me. He met me there. He always does. I began to understand that there is always more to experience with Jesus.

What do you need to be set free from? Whatever it is, the situation is not hopeless. The tomb is empty, and Jesus is alive. You don't have to be a victim; you can have victory. You are not the sum total of your consequences; you are a conqueror. You are not defined by your failures; you are forgiven and free. You are not your mistakes; you are made new in Jesus. It's not only about what you have done or what has happened to you; it is about what Jesus wants to do for you, in you, and through you.

We will talk about this more in the next chapter, but I would like you to consider what agreements you have made about yourself that need to be broken. Have you agreed that you are not enough and have something to prove? My own experience has been that the more I feel I have "something to prove," the more I need to *experience* more of Jesus in my own life and story. There are always more agreements to be broken. A big part of learning to live free is learning to break the agreements and pray the blood of Jesus and the unconditional love of the Father into those spaces in our lives. The good news is that there is always more to experience with Jesus.

Winston Churchill is quoted as saying, "You will never reach your destination if you stop and throw stones at every dog that barks." I can't help but think of all the years that my life in Christ had been stalled by my stopping to throw stones at and prove those barking dogs wrong. I had lived my entire life determined to show "them." What's ironic is that I am not really sure who "them" was. This has been a long, hard journey for me, and I am hopeful that my sharing it will make your journey shorter and easier. I have experienced tremendous healing and seen marked improvement, and now more frequently I choose to sit in the space of being a beloved son with nothing to prove. Most of the time. Sometimes, I still need to be reminded.

Beloved Sons and Daughters

About six months ago, I was having lunch with my mentor and good friend Jon Petersen. On that particular day, I was whining a little more than usual about the problems and challenges that we face here at DCC. I'll admit, it wasn't my best moment: "Blah, blah, blah, COVID wreaked havoc, people walked away when we decided to do an eight-week series on God's heart for all people, and financially things have been and continue to be really challenging for us." You know what I am talking about, right? Somebody call a "waaaaambulance." As I whined and complained, Jon nodded and listened lovingly and patiently, as he always does. When I was finished, we sat in silence for a few minutes, which is typical with Jon. Finally, he said, "Buddy, here's what I want for you. Rather than you riding the waves, the ups and downs, the highs and lows, I want you to rest in being a beloved son. If God has given you the vision, he will bring the how. You need to rest in being a beloved son." There it was again. Just a beloved son with absolutely nothing to prove. I find myself needing to be reminded of that. It is only the continuing daily experience and work of Jesus in my life that will help me arrive and stay there.

To some extent, we are all on a journey moving from being an invalidated person with something to prove to being a beloved child with absolutely nothing to prove. The enemy wants to keep us in this "something to prove" space. A big part of truly experiencing Jesus is learning to let go of that. A big part of experiencing Jesus is learning to lean hard into what Paul reminded us of in 2 Corinthians 6:18: above all else, God is our Father, and we are his beloved sons and daughters. As John said in 1 John 3, the Father's great love has been "lavished on us, that we should be called children of God" (v. 1).

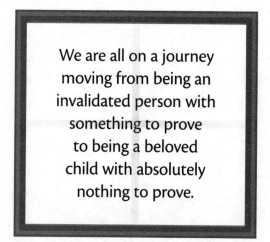

We are all on a journey
moving from being an
invalidated person with
something to prove
to being a beloved
child with absolutely
nothing to prove.

One last thing before we leave this. God's Word is not the only way to experience God. Music and worship are other ways. I recognize that music may not be your thing, and that's okay. You may not be a worship junkie like me; I get it. I still want to challenge you to try this on for size. It really helps me, and I think it will help you. The lyrics from the following two songs help me experience Jesus. The first is one of my favorite worship songs, "Jireh," by Elevation Worship and Maverick City Music. The word *Jireh* means "the Lord will provide." I have a wall hanging that I see when I step out of bed each morning that says, "Jireh, You Are Enough."

While I encourage you to just sit and soak in the entire song, these are the lyrics that are particularly relevant here.

> I'm already loved
> I'm already chosen
> I know who I am

I know what You've spoken
I'm already loved
More than I could imagine
And that is enough.[3]

You are already loved more than you can imagine.

Do that, and then soak in the lyrics from "I Am Your Beloved" by Jonathan David and Melissa Helser, specifically these:

I am your beloved, You have bought me with
        Your blood
And on Your hand You've written out my name
I am Your beloved, one the Father loves
Mercy has defeated all my shame.
The One who knows me best
Is the One who loves me most.
There is nothing I have done
That could change the Father's love.[4]

The more that we experience—not know or know about, but *experience*—Jesus, the less we have to prove. When we feel this "something to prove" drive stirring and rising up in us, it indicates a need to experience more Jesus in our lives and stories. Trust me, it's true. The one who knows you best is the one who loves you most. Let go of the pressure. You have nothing to prove.

— 7 —

The Rest of the Story

"I thought that I was too far gone for everything I've done wrong. Yeah, I'm the one who dug this grave. But you called my name, you called my name."

Lauren Daigle, "Still Rolling Stones"

---◆---

When I was growing up, we listened to the radio quite a bit. I remember hearing Paul Harvey's radio show, called *The Rest of the Story*, in the car driving with the family. Like all great communicators, Harvey spent the first part of the story building tension. Then, he would go to a commercial break before returning and resolving the tension, always ending with "And now you know the rest of the story."

With Christians, I'm not sure that is true. I think that we have missed a significant part of the story. It wasn't until I blew up my life that I discovered what I had been missing, not only the rest of my own story, but the rest of the God story. It is the rest of the God story that makes the discovery of the rest of our own stories so important and life-changing for us.

Religious and Restless

Missing the rest of our stories is common. Missing the rest of the God story is too. We see that in the story of Nicodemus, a religious guy who seemed to know that something was not quite right in his life (John 3:1–21). Despite his religious ways, Nicodemus came to Jesus at night to talk, looking for the rest of the story. Nicodemus was no ordinary guy. He was a Pharisee, a member of the Jewish ruling council, and highly esteemed in that culture.

By the time Jesus hit the scene, the Jewish faith had been hijacked by religious guys like Nicodemus. Somewhere along the way, they lost the aspect of the faith that was about having a personal relationship with God and exchanged it for a faith that was all about rules, regulations, posture, and position. When you read the Bible, you can see that every hostile encounter Jesus had was with religious guys like this. But this encounter was different. Nicodemus had bought into the idea that being at the top of the religious food chain was the ultimate destination in Jewish life, and yet he was feeling empty. Nicodemus came to Jesus because, despite his religious life, something deep inside remained unsettled.

Similar to Nicodemus, many of us have been in church for a long time, and yet something is still not quite right, something remains unsettled. We've got religion, the robe, the titles, the rules and regulations,

Sunday school, Wednesday-night church, the books of the Bible memorized, our small group, Bible reading, worship songs, tithing, sermons, a quiet time, a regular Christian podcast cued up, K-Love on the radio, and even seminary training, but something is still missing.

When Jesus told Nicodemus he had to be born again, Nicodemus was confused. I think I would be too. Jesus tried to help him understand, and a part of his explanation is found in the two verses that precede John 3:16. Jesus said:

> Just as Moses lifted up the snake in the desert, so the
> Son of Man must be lifted up, that everyone who
> believes in him may have eternal life. (John 3:14–15)

Jesus was referring to the passage in Numbers where the Israelites sort of thumbed their noses at God, so God allowed poisonous snakes to come into their camp and bite them. Lots of people started dying. God told Moses to fashion a brass snake, put it on a pole, and lift it up. Those who looked at the snake on a pole would be healed. But here's the rest of the story. Just like that image of a snake wrapped around a stick, Jesus came to be our healer, restorer, redeemer, and rescuer. There is something to this MASH unit thinking. Everything about the image Jesus uses says not salvation, but rescue. Jesus said, "Here I am right in front of you and yet you don't really see me." Why not? Lots of stuff is blocking our view.

There is so much goofy stuff going on today in the name of Jesus. I am not being critical of the church. The people in it are for the most part very sincere. Sometimes, though, they are sincerely goofy. They are sincerely goofy people with good intentions who are all about organs, pianos, fog machines, big hair, no hair, reverent tones, dog barks, snake handling, robes, funny hats, funny smells, little bells, golden altars, and velvet chairs. They are people who even speak a different language. I am not talking about tongues. (If you have that gift, go for it.) I am talking about the words Christians throw around as though they should make sense, things like: drunk in the Spirit, thee, thou, washed in the blood, soaking in the Word. Normal people don't talk like that. God loves them, and bless all of their little hearts, but isn't it true? Some of the most spiritual people you and I know are not people we want to hang out or have dinner with.

Most of us have yet to experience the rest of the story. There is a difference between knowing, knowing about, and really experiencing Jesus. We are not sure how Nicodemus responded to Jesus, but the question isn't what Nicodemus did with or about Jesus. The question is, what will we do?

Just like Nicodemus, we too are often missing all that Jesus came to do for us. I was a forty-year-old pastor who had been in church his entire life. I was teaching the Bible every single week while at the very same time continuing to miss it. What am I talking about? What have we missed? What is the rest of the story? I thought you would never ask.

Rescue, Not Religion

John 3:16 is not a mystery to us in the church. It's known and we know that we are hopeless without it. The *rest* of the story is found in Luke chapter 4. I didn't discover this until almost three years after I had blown up my life. We can't afford to miss it. Let's pick it up in verse 14.

> Jesus returned to Galilee in the power of the Spirit, and news about him spread through the whole countryside. He was teaching in their synagogues, and everyone praised him.
>
> He went to Nazareth, where he had been brought up, and on the Sabbath day he went into the synagogue, as was his custom. He stood up to read. (Luke 4:14–16)

It's what Jesus chose to read in this situation that is most significant. But first, let's recognize the significance of who he chose to read it to. Jesus was with the people who chose to go to synagogue on the Sabbath. His message that day was not for people who were uninterested in God, but for the people who were chasing after God, the people who knew the most Scripture and had the best understanding of what God expected of them.

These were also religious people from Jesus' hometown who had watched Jesus grow up! They had thirty years of exposure to Jesus, so they were the people who knew him best. Now let that sink in for a second. What comes with that type of exposure? Expectations. In fact, I think that is why Jesus chose to address this specific group. Despite what they may have heard, it is likely that Jesus really did need to blow up the expectations and limitations that they were placing on him as the carpenter Joseph's son.

One of the kindest things Jesus can do for any of us is to blow up the expectations and limitations we have placed on him in our own lives. For me, it came at one of the most tragic, darkest, and most hopeless moments of my life. I was introduced to John Eldredge's *Wild at Heart* when the book was first published in 2001. A good pastor friend, Eddie, gave me the book and told me that, when he read the book, he thought of me. At the time, I was a volunteer coleading a singles' ministry with Eddie in the huge church we were attending while I was still practicing law. I read it, thought it was a really good book for men, and shelved it.

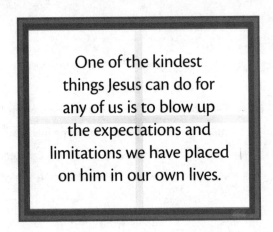

One of the kindest things Jesus can do for any of us is to blow up the expectations and limitations we have placed on him in our own lives.

I didn't pick it back up again until after I lost my ministry. There I sat in my sin. My world got strangely quiet. People didn't know what to do or what to say, and so most chose to run away and say nothing. Finally, a friend, Michael, took me back to and through the book *Wild at Heart*. Reading through it a second time, John's comment that 95 percent of affairs have nothing to do with sex caused my heart to jump. Maybe there was hope for me. Maybe there was an explanation for what I had done. Maybe there was more to this than just temptation and sin.

It was the beginning of my journey to a place I had never gone before, the rest of my story. About a year later, I was sitting at a Wild at Heart Boot Camp in Buena Vista, Colorado, listening to John Eldredge unpack and teach this passage from Luke 4. Let's go to verse 17.

> And the scroll of the prophet Isaiah was handed to him. Unrolling it, he found the place where it is written:
>
> "The Spirit of the Lord is on me,
>   because he has anointed me
>   to proclaim good news to the poor.
> He has sent me to proclaim freedom for the
>   prisoners
>   and recovery of sight for the blind,
> to set the oppressed free,
>   to proclaim the year of the Lord's favor."
>   (Luke 4:17–19)

Luke seems to have given a summary of everything that Isaiah said in the first three verses of chapter 61. Isaiah also included healing of broken hearts; comfort for those who mourn and grieve; and turning ashes into beauty, mourning into joy, and despair into praise. These are not categories of people in need of forgiveness but places of need in every one of our lives and stories. Jesus was pointing to everything he came to do for us. He was addressing what I believe to be one of the greatest gaps, one of the biggest missing pieces, in the church today—the rest of the story.

When I crashed, the most common conclusion reached about me by church people who experienced it or heard about it was that I was just a bad person. I don't blame them. When we are unaware of our invisible lives, our stories, it is difficult, if not impossible, to reach any other conclusion. What I began to understand was that maybe I was not a bad person after all. Maybe I was a really broken person who did a terribly bad thing. There is a difference. I started to discover that the secrets behind the worst decisions and mistakes I had ever made in my life were tucked deeply within my story. So, when I hit rock bottom, I began to devour the book *Wild at Heart*. As I read, the words jumped off the page. I would often shout them to Stacy in the other room. I will never forget shouting to her one day as I was reading on the porcelain throne. I said, "Stacy, I get it. I have spent all these years wrongly taking my question of 'Do I really have what it takes to be a man?' to you and expecting you to answer it." How could I have missed all of this for so many years of my life? My approach was misplaced. I should have been taking my questions not to Stacy, but to Jesus.

Suddenly, I began to have hope. There was so much more that Jesus wanted to do and needed to do in my heart, life, and story. I'm not minimizing my sin or any other sin. It is our sin that nailed Jesus to the cross. But I had not missed that. I had missed the rest of the story. I had missed what Jesus himself said in Luke 4. He came to heal, redeem, restore, bring freedom, to set our captive hearts free. Suddenly, the rest of the story began to change my life. My life would never, ever be the same. Just a few years into my desert experience, out of ministry, churches started inquiring about my future. I believed, despite the naysayers who told me that I would never be in ministry again (or if I would, that God wouldn't bless it), that God was telling me we were going to do this again, but differently this time. This message of story and rescue and all that Jesus came to do for us would be the foundation of the church I would lead in the future.

The Path to Freedom

In the eight amazing years I had with Craig McConnell, I learned that the very best thing I could do for Discovery Church was to walk with God and take care of my own heart, to continue to walk into my own story, and to allow Jesus to continue to heal, redeem, and restore the broken places in me. Better than any possible class, program, or system, the very best thing I can possibly do as the leader of this place is to stay in my own story with Jesus. There is always more that Jesus wants and needs to do there.

To this day God continues to build this tribe called Discovery Church on that message. It doesn't make us better, but it does make us different. It also makes things messy at times. Our mission is to help people discover their stories, experience Jesus, and live to rescue. By definition, that is an extremely messy mission, but there is so much life in it. Let's finish the story, Luke 4:20–21.

> Then he rolled up the scroll, gave it back to the
> attendant and sat down. The eyes of everyone in the
> synagogue were fastened on him. He began by saying

to them, "Today this scripture is fulfilled in your hearing."

It's the ultimate "mic-drop moment," isn't it? Jesus said, "Make no mistake about it. This is talking about me. This is what I came to do." Yeah, it starts with forgiveness, but it is so much bigger than that. Jesus came to heal, redeem, restore, repair our brokenness, set our captive hearts free, and lead us to the life to the fullest that he came to bring us. So, ask yourself, "Is that the Jesus that I have experienced in my life?" Remember, there is a difference between living forgiven and living free. Are you living free? Most Christians I know are not. Something has to change.

I grew up in a church full of people committed to living religious lives full of knowledge, duty, obligation, and obedience. I grew up doing the same. Honestly, I don't know why. The people in that church appeared to be pretty stiff and miserable. I grew up following that trend, because it was all I knew to do. But that life left me empty. I always could hear a voice speaking to me suggesting that there was something missing in all of it. I can't prove it, but I think that voice spoke to my dad too. My dad was different. He was loved, but he never really fit in at that church. I guess I really am my father's son. My dad was a blue-collar basketball coach who drank wine on rare occasion, much to my mom's chagrin, smoked cigars at work on the loading dock with his guys, and told some jokes that church people would have frowned upon.

I'm not saying every decision my dad made was the right one, but I am saying that he loved Jesus. My dad often worked nights. I will never forget him lying in his bed, reading from that old King James Bible before falling asleep. His old Bible is one of my favorite possessions to this day. No, he couldn't quote or teach the Bible like others in the church and was even afraid to pray publicly. But somehow, somehow, my dad figured out how to live it. My dad passed away about twenty years ago, so we never really got a chance to talk about all of this. I watched him refuse to settle for a religious life full of duty, obligation, and obedience. I'm convinced that my dad understood this. There's a difference between living forgiven and living free, and he wanted both. We all do.

One of the biggest tragedies in the church today is that so many of us have missed the rest of the story. We have unknowingly settled for some smaller percentage of the life that is available to us, are doing our time until Jesus comes back, and have lost or are losing heart. Proverbs 4:23 says that above all else we need to guard our hearts since they are the wellsprings of life. In other words, our hearts are the sources of this abundant life that Jesus came to provide. There is more, and something inside each of us knows it. We want to live free. The tattoo on my left arm says, in Aramaic, "me too." In other words, I too have a jacked-up story. The rest of the tattoo says "live free." Between those two phrases is a unique cross. Yes, I have a jacked-up story, but because of all that Jesus has done and continues to do in my life, I live free. The story of your life is the long and sustained assault upon your heart by the one who knows who you could be and fears you. This is the rest of your story. If we continue to overlook or miss the rest of our stories, we will never live free.

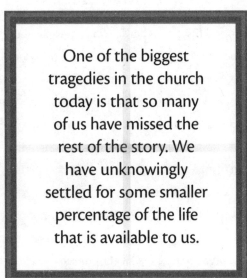

One of the biggest
tragedies in the church
today is that so many
of us have missed the
rest of the story. We
have unknowingly
settled for some smaller
percentage of the life
that is available to us.

Rescued from Shame

As we move into the rest of the story and seek healing, redemption, and restoration, let's call it what it is: the rescue of Jesus. We must recognize this. Our shame is a big deal. Whenever I would screw up as a kid, my grandmother would say, "Gregory Allen, you ought to be ashamed of yourself. Shame on you." "Shame on you" is a common phrase, but I think we use this phrase without understanding the significance of what we are saying. If we really understood the power of shame, we would be careful wishing it on anyone.

A few years back, a friend gave me a book by a board-certified Christian psychiatrist named Curt Thompson called *The Soul of Shame: Retelling the Stories We Believe about Ourselves*. Now, I love books, and gifts is my primary love language, so for me it was a fastball down the middle. But I have to be honest. I remember thinking, *Cool,*

I want to read it. It might be helpful for others. But I have been working on my own junk and story for fourteen years now, and I've got a handle on this story and shame stuff. I couldn't have been more wrong. One of the primary weapons in the enemy's arsenal is shame. So many of our stories, and to some extent all of them, have been written in the language of shame. As Curt Thompson said, shame makes its way into all of our stories at an early age.[1]

What does this look like in your life and story today? How far back can you trace it? What are you most ashamed of in your life and story? It may not be something you have done. Shame comes just as powerfully with things that have been said to, said about, and done to us. My intention is not to bring more heaviness or hopelessness on you. That's never the goal. I do want you to pay attention to your resistance and hesitancy to even go there and the heaviness that you feel as you attempt to do that. It points to the power and significance of shame in our lives. There's no question, it's there. The question is, what have we done with it? The answer for most of us—yes, even most of us Christians—is not much. Something has got to change.

The truth is that most of us do exactly what Adam and Eve did in Genesis 3. We hide in response to our shame. We feel enormous pressure to hide the things that bring us shame. In Adam and Eve's story, when the enemy approached them, they were sinless. If Adam and Eve were overwhelmed with shame after one mistake, don't you think that we are going to be overwhelmed with shame in all of our mistakes too? When you think about all that has happened over the course of our lives and stories, the enemy has a lot more to work with than he did with Adam and Eve. He brings shame, and our response is to hide. Adam and Eve hid from God, and we hide the source of that shame from all the people around us. Unfortunately, it often feels like there is not another option. There is. Listen to this in Hebrews 12:2–3.

> Fixing our eyes on Jesus, the pioneer and perfecter of faith. For the joy set before him he endured the cross, scorning its shame, and sat down at the right hand of the throne of God. Consider him who endured such opposition from sinners, so that you will not grow weary and lose heart.

Jesus scorned the *shame* of the cross. The Greek word for *scorned* here is *kataphroneo*, which means "to despise, look down on, take on, render powerless, put in its proper place." This is a key point if we really want to experience all the life that Jesus came to bring us. It is a significant part of the rest of the story.

While our sin is covered, shame continues. If we are followers of Jesus, our sin has been buried as deep as the deepest sea. God remembers it no more. But shame remains a powerful tool in the hands of our enemy. On our own, we are no match for the enemy and the shame he burdens us with. But with the Spirit and power of Jesus that live inside of us, he is no match for us. "Greater is he that is in you, than he that is in the world" (1 John 4:4 KJV). Jesus not only allowed his body to be broken and his blood poured out for us on the cross, he also rendered shame powerless. However, it is one thing to say we believe that and a completely different thing to live our lives every day as if it's true. Here's how Curt Thompson described it: "Every minute of every day we must choose between shame and love."[2]

We must learn to lean into the rest of the story. We must learn to choose love, not shame. We must learn to rest in what Jesus did on the cross. He not only conquered sin, but rendered our shame powerless too. A big step is to quietly name our shame to Jesus while envisioning him right in front of us, looking him in the eyes, feeling his hug and love, and hearing what he says to be true about us. What would life look like if all the shaming voices were silenced and God's voice was the only voice that we heard? Yes, you have been forgiven, but have you really and truly experienced all that Jesus came to do for you? Has your captive heart been set free?

Last year, I was listening to a podcast by my good buddy Morgan Snyder over at Wild at Heart. At the end of the podcast, he prayed. The prayer moved me so much that I went back and listened to it again, stopping after each line so that I could transcribe it. I don't think there is a better place for us to end this chapter, this important part of our journey together. I don't know that there is a better way for us to step into the rest of the story. I hope it does for your heart what it continues to do for mine. I would encourage you not to just read it, but to begin to pray this prayer regularly over yourself, your life, your story.

"Jesus, I am struck afresh that the real work you are doing is restoring the true me. Father, I want to be curious about what you set in my heart that has gone underground, that is hidden, that is self-protected out of valid harm. You say in the Scriptures that, here in this river, you will turn our old life into a kingdom life, that you will ignite a life of fire within us through the Holy Spirit, and that you will change and transform us from the inside out, over time, steadily, piece by piece, and part by part. You will cleanse the house, making a sweep of our lives. That you will give us

the courage to become more and more aware of the false, and that you would become more of the safe place in order that we can dismantle the false and restore the true self.

God, you are my refuge and safe place. I have nothing to fear in being found. You rescue me from hidden traps. Because you are my refuge, I have nothing to fear. Because you provide what I need, I find myself without lack. Because in you, the true me is more than enough and is without lack. I can come in a soul safe space to be exposed. To become aware of my true self. Dismantle the false, and restore everything that you meant when you meant me. I trust you, God, and I trust that, because I am your child, I am on time today. And I trust that you are with me working right where I am, right in this place of who I have become. Fill me, God, with your light and with your life. Shine your light, be my life, expose what you want to expose. I invite you into my true self, to excavate, to heal, and to show me what's in the way. In Jesus' name. Amen."[3]

— 8 —

Different

"Get used to different."

Jesus, from *The Chosen*

———◆———

I have always loved movies. Movies like *Braveheart, Gladiator, We Were Soldiers, Unbroken,* and *Hacksaw Ridge* are some of my favorites. They inspire me to think about the story I am living and who I want to be. Despite that, I have always been skeptical of Christian movies and television series. *The Passion of the Christ* was one of the rare exceptions to that hesitation. Don't hear me wrong. I am not against them. It's just that, despite my love for Jesus and desire for the story to be told in every way possible, Christian movies and TV shows often just don't move me like others do. No worries, God once spoke through a donkey in the Old Testament, and although I have my own cracks and flaws, he speaks through me at times too. I'm convinced that he uses Christian movies and shows too, regardless of what I think. That still doesn't mean that I have to watch them, and I usually opt out.

All that to say, when *The Chosen* series first came out, I quickly concluded it would be just like the others, and I opted out. That changed when my friend Wes gave me a T-shirt that said "Get used to different." He said it was a line from *The Chosen*, when Jesus was calling Matthew, the tax collector, to follow him. Tax collectors were Jewish people who sold out to the Roman authorities to collect taxes for Rome and were typically hated by their own people. In this scene, Simon (Peter), who was standing next to Jesus when he called Matthew, whispered, "Are you sure? This is different." Jesus turned to him and said, "Get used to different." In other words, "Believing in me is one thing. Following me is often going to look, feel, and be different." I have to admit that I was wrong in my original decision to write off *The Chosen*. Once I saw how Jesus was depicted in that scene, I had to see more. Stacy and I decided to watch the entire series, and I fall more in love with Jesus with every episode.

Revolutionary, Not Religious

Life with Jesus is different. The life that Jesus invited his disciples into was far different from any religious life they had been taught, experienced, or heard about. That is just as true for most of us in our world today too. There is a difference between believing in Jesus, knowing about Jesus, and loving Jesus, and really and truly experiencing Jesus. Once we have experienced Jesus in all the ways we are exploring in this book—his forgiveness, healing, redemption, restoration, and rescue—we should be different. Experiencing Jesus should leave us different. Jesus said that we, his sheep, hear his voice and follow him (John 10:27). John said if we claim to believe in him, we must walk as he walked (1 John 2:6). Ask yourself, "As people experience me, is there any real evidence that I have experienced and am continuing to experience Jesus?" Let's talk about some of the challenges we face with that.

In *The Chosen*, when Jesus said, "Get used to different," he was saying, "Peter, I'm not okay with you not being okay with him." Jesus is not okay with us being not okay with people in the world around us either. We often struggle with that. As I am writing this chapter, the story of Damar Hamlin is fresh in the news. He plays safety for the NFL's Buffalo Bills. In a much anticipated matchup between the Buffalo Bills and the Cincinnati Bengals in January 2023, Hamlin made what appeared to be a routine tackle, stood to his feet, adjusted his face mask, then collapsed on the field. Medical personnel immediately ran onto the field, administered CPR, and finally resuscitated Hamlin, restored his heartbeat, and then rushed him to the hospital. His heart stopped a second time when he reached the hospital, and he had to be resuscitated again. None of the players on the field knew how to respond. There was a lot of angst, fear, worry, and tears, even after Hamlin was taken away by ambulance. They all just needed to know that their brother was going to be okay. Honestly, I couldn't stop watching the coverage. I needed to know that too.

The great news is that he was okay. Because of the heroic efforts of medical personnel, both on the field and at the hospital, Damar Hamlin recovered from his cardiac arrest and is once again with the Bills. When he was first taken off sedation after his injury, he was still on a breathing tube and couldn't speak, so he grabbed a notepad and wrote down a question: "Did we win?" I absolutely love that. What a warrior, competitor, and teammate!

During the TV coverage on the night that Hamlin collapsed, people started to throw around the formerly taboo word *prayer*. There were so many people who, stunned and not really knowing what to say, went with "We need to pray for Damar and his family." It became a central theme. "Pray for Damar #3" was all over everything, everywhere, including social media throughout the entire week.

People from all walks of life, belief systems, backgrounds, and allegiances to various NFL teams were moving toward each other, coming together to try to rally this young man back to health. It was a beautiful thing to see and experience, and yet it seemed like a countercultural experience in the cancel-culture world we live in today, a world where if you disagree with me, for all practical purposes, you are dead to me. I couldn't help but think that maybe we were beginning to break new ground. Why does this have to be an isolated incident? Why can't we default to this daily moving forward? If we can rise above our differences, move toward each other, and come together for the benefit of this young man, Damar Hamlin, in his moment of need, why can't we rise above our differences moving forward? It shouldn't take tragedy to take us there. We can disagree with each other and still love each other. If we embrace that as followers of Jesus, we will be, and bring, the change our world so desperately needs. As Christians, we should be leading the way. Too often, we're not.

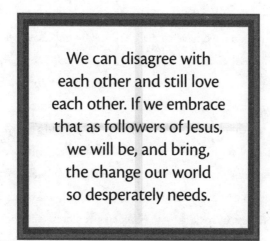

We can disagree with each other and still love each other. If we embrace that as followers of Jesus, we will be, and bring, the change our world so desperately needs.

Daring to Be Different

What would happen if Christians led the way and started living today with a focus on the equal worth, value, and dignity of all people all the time? It's not about waiting on the world to change. It is about being the change that needs to happen in this world. Something needs to change, and that change is on us. Experiencing Jesus means becoming more like Jesus. We must understand, embrace, and live out God's heart. His heart is for the rescue, redemption, and restoration of all people. It always has been, and it always will be. In the Old Testament, God chose Israel to help with the rescue of all people. Things began to break down when they started equating being chosen with being privileged. What naturally comes from that is feelings of superiority and the idea that God prefers some people over others. Unfortunately, this way of thinking is still prevalent in Christians today. We have a way of writing people off. That must change.

As Christians, we have to get back to the God story, starting in Genesis 1:27. All of us, men, women, all races, all people, have been created in the image of God, and all of our blood connects us back to Adam and Eve. Biblically speaking, there is one race, and yet race is something that divides us every day. It shouldn't, especially as Christians, especially in the church. What God did in Genesis was radical. In every other Ancient Near Eastern creation account, people were created to be slaves to the gods. God instead said that we are created in his image, as royalty, with equal value, worth, and dignity. This is why, when God came to Abraham in Genesis 12 to initiate his plan of rescue, he not only commissioned him as the father of the people of Israel but proclaimed that all families and nations on earth would be blessed through him. God's heart is for the rescue, redemption, and restoration of *all* people. The apostle Paul gave us some additional insight in Ephesians 2, beginning with verse 13:

> But now in Christ Jesus you who once were far away
> have been brought near by the blood of Christ.
>   For he himself is our peace, who has made the two
> groups one and has destroyed the barrier, the dividing

wall of hostility, by setting aside in his flesh the law
with its commands and regulations. (vv. 13–15)

This is what life is supposed to look like on this side of the cross. Not only can we all trace our heritage back through one bloodline to Adam, one blood—the blood of Jesus—changed and continues to change everything. The blood of Jesus allows those who are far from God to be close to God. Jesus destroyed the dividing wall of hostility. Yes, he came to save us and make sure that we can have and hold a ticket to heaven someday, but it is so much bigger than that. Jesus came to break down all the walls that divide us. Here's the question: How much am I like Jesus in how I respond to people who are different from me?

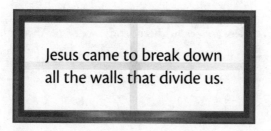

Jesus came to break down
all the walls that divide us.

Stacy and I have a small plaque hanging in the hall outside our bedroom. I see it every morning when I walk out. It's a quote from Mahatma Gandhi: "You must be the change you wish to see in the world." We Christians must be the change that we want to see in the world. We do that one person at a time. Let's decide today to start being the change this world needs and pray that God will open our eyes to see all the things, past and present, that break his heart. Let's pray that he would help us be the people he created us to be, so that his light and hope will be seen and experienced by all people in the world around us and through us. We tend to build walls between us. Experiencing Jesus involves learning to tear them all down. Let's talk about how we can begin to do that.

Let's jump into this part of the journey with a question: What are Christians most known for? Or to put it another way: Christians are full of _____. How would you complete that sentence? How would people in the world complete it? I don't know about you, but for me, words like *hypocrisy, judgment, hate, condemnation, self-righteousness*, and *irrelevance* come to mind.

Here's another question. What should the answer be? Let's see if we can get some clarity from John 1:14.

> The Word became flesh and made his dwelling among us. We have seen his glory, the glory of the one and only Son, who came from the Father, full of grace and truth.

John starts with the *Word* that is becoming flesh. The Word in this context is Jesus. God stepped into the story he is writing—the story we are living in—in the form of Jesus, who is fully God and fully man. But how does God enter the story? The Greek word translated "full" is *pleres*. It means "completely occupied, filled to the brim, totally full." Jesus came completely full of grace and completely full of truth. Which means that we, as followers of Jesus, should be known as people of unlimited grace too. Not only that, *church* should be known as a place of full-on and full-out grace too. If only it were that easy. Unfortunately, we all have our grace limits. Where we are drawing our "grace lines" is a very important question.

Several years ago, we at DCC taught through a series called "The Separation of Church and Hate." In that series, we talked about a very common place where we Christians tend to draw the grace line in our world today. It is with the LGBTQIA+ (lesbian, gay, bisexual, transgender, questioning or queer, intersex, asexual, and others) community.

Before I say more, let me say this. There is so much great stuff out there on this subject that I would encourage you to read. I would start with *Redeeming Sex: Naked Conversations about Sexuality and Spirituality* by Debra Hirsch, *Us versus Us: The Untold Story of Religion and the LGBT Community* by Andrew Marin, *Brimstone: The Art and Act of Holy Nonjudgment* by Hugh Halter, *Messy Grace* and *Messy Truth* by Caleb Kaltenbach, and quite frankly, anything and everything written by Preston Sprinkle. That dude is brilliant. Don't take my word for any of this. Study and read up on it for yourself.

Grace Limits

Here's the challenge. There is a dynamic that plays out in most of our "Christian" lives that goes something like this. We extend grace to the extent we can understand or relate to what the person in need of grace is dealing with. If something reaches the point where we can't really understand it or relate to it, because we ourselves don't struggle with it, we tend to draw a hard line there. The grace often stops there, doesn't it? We all tend to have our grace limits.

Years ago, I reached out to a mentor of mine, one of the men who saw the call of God on my life when I was still a practicing trial attorney and ended up being very instrumental in helping me transition into ministry after ten years of practicing law. While we had not spoken in years, I reached out because he had just "come out"—he had just publicly revealed that he was transgender. By the time I heard about it (from some other Christians who were mocking and laughing about it), she had already changed her name and her voice and was living as a female. Some of us are struggling with the use of the pronoun *she* here. If that is you, I get it. Check yourself, and hang with me.

Most in the church community had reached their grace limit with my friend. I have to admit that it was awkward for me too. But I had a decision to make. I had no idea what I would say or what to do, but I knew I had to reach out and have a conversation with her. So, I sent a text, she responded, and we set up a phone call. In the minutes leading up to that call, I began to panic. I could not understand or relate to what she was going through and was afraid of saying something completely stupid or somehow making things worse. Something inside me wanted to avoid the conversation, make up an excuse, and just not call. As I was sitting there thinking of bailing, I realized that I was being tempted to draw the line and limit God's grace. Suddenly, in that moment, I flashed back to the low point in my own life when that leader from my previous church told me I was outside the grace of God. So no, I couldn't understand or relate, and I had no idea what to say, but I was not going to allow her to believe that there was a limit to God's grace. I walked away from that experience determined to make this my question: When people experience me, is it even remotely close to an experience with Jesus?

Jesus has unlimited grace. The church should be a place of unlimited grace as well, but too often, it just isn't. About twelve years ago, we had a guy whose life was tanking show up on a Sunday morning at DCC. He was high on crystal meth. That morning, he happened to start talking to a guy named Brandon. During the conversation he admitted to Brandon that he was high. Do you know what Brandon's immediate response was? "I am glad you are here." Brandon and his wife, Blanca, invited him over to their house that day. Weeks later, as the guy was telling me this story, he broke down and began to sob. He said, "One question. I only have one question. Who does that? I mean, here I am high on meth, and this dude invites me over to be around his wife, his kids, and his stuff. Most people wouldn't even want me to know where they lived. Who does that?" Answer: Jesus does that. It's unlimited grace, and it's totally freakin' contagious.

One more story before we move on. When I arrived to be a part of DCC in 2008, we were a church of eighty to a hundred people. New people really stood out. We rarely had to worry about that, though. We were a struggling, failing, five-year-old church plant, and people in the area had already concluded, "Yeah, been there done that." One of the first new people to show up in my first few months at the church was Tim. Tim made himself somewhat unforgettable by the T-shirt he wore one day. It said, "Dip me in chocolate and throw me in a room full of lesbians." I didn't get to talk with him that day, but someone told me about his shirt. When I caught up with him the following week, he told me that his buddy Jeremy, who he worked with, had invited him to church. He then said, "Last week was a test. Jeremy said this is a safe place, so I intentionally wore that T-shirt to test you." I was like, "Oh yeah? How did we do? Anyone say anything to you?" He said, "I only heard one comment. 'Nice shirt.'" Unlimited grace.

We need to be honest with ourselves. God doesn't categorize people, but we often do. We categorize sin and then categorize people by the sin they struggle with. I know, because I have been the victim of that. When I had an affair, I got dropped into a certain category by certain pastors and church people. I remain in that category with some still today. It sucks. If you are experiencing that as you sit here today, I am sorry. Unfortunately, it happens a lot. We read passages like Leviticus 18 and 20, Romans 1, 1 Corinthians 6, and 1 Timothy 1, and we come to quick and certain conclusions about people. We drop them into specific categories, and suddenly, the church is no longer a safe place for them.

I love this quote by Debra Hirsch: "Acknowledging our own broken sexuality enables us to identify with a sexually broken humanity.... We must see heterosexuals as no less broken (and in need of salvation) than homosexuals. We are all together in the human experience of life and trying to live out the reality of the kingdom.... Every human being on the planet is sexually broken. Everybody's orientation is disoriented. All of us are on a journey toward wholeness; not one of us is excluded."[1]

As Christians, we need to stop relying on our pastor's teaching or our church's position on this stuff, and study it for ourselves. And regardless of how much we have or have not studied, our response should always be the same. One of my favorite Billy Graham moments was when he attended a rally in support of President Bill Clinton after the big sex scandal had become public. He was asked by a reporter why he was there supporting the president after all that he had done to his family and this country. Graham said, "It's the Holy Spirit's job to convict, God's job to judge, and my job to love." The question for Christians is, are we focused on our job?

Our only agenda as Christians should be that every person who bumps into us experiences the radical and reckless love of Jesus. Yes, there is mystery, confusion, and misunderstanding, but if we are willing to fill the gaps with love, grace, truth, and compassion, with God's help, we can sort it all out. We are not asked to condone or to condemn. We are meant to have compassionate conversations with people of all types. Experiencing Jesus means becoming more like Jesus. Love and unlimited grace pave the way for truth.

Truth Adjustments

So, we've talked about grace. Let's shift gears now and talk about truth. Jesus was full of grace and full of uncompromising truth. If that's true, then this should also be true: Christians should be known as people of uncompromising truth. We are so much more comfortable with this part of the equation, aren't we? The Bible says it, we believe it, that settles it. Truth tends to be our central focus in the church, but *uncompromising* means unadjusted. We claim to be all about truth, but aren't we all guilty of adjusting truth in one way or another? I know I am.

I have found myself saying things like, "Wait a minute, God. I am not completely comfortable with that. I don't really like that part. I think I will skip over that or find a way that it doesn't really apply to me." Compromising truth never leads us to the life that we are looking for, and yet, it is exactly what we do. But the moment we start ignoring parts of God's truth is the moment that God's Word becomes one more self-help, try-harder, believe-in-yourself, partial-truth book or magazine that you can buy near the checkout at any grocery store. "Yeah, Jesus offers great advice, just like Oprah and Dr. Phil. You can take it or leave it." We must learn to be people of uncompromising truth, even when that truth is hard to hear and even harder to apply to our lives. Jesus was full of grace and truth. As we experience Jesus, we should be too.

Back to my earlier question. Christians are full of _____. What should the answer be? How about "grace and truth"? Not limited grace and adjusted truth. Not 80 percent grace and 20 percent truth, or 40 percent grace and 60 percent truth or some other wacked combination of the two. It's not either-or. It's 100 percent grace and 100 percent truth all the time. I'm not suggesting it's easy, but I am suggesting that, as Christians, it is nonnegotiable for us. Experiencing Jesus should mean that every day we become more like Jesus.

In August 2008, I was hired to be the pastor of DCC, and our family moved from North Carolina to Colorado. Discovery had been in serious decline for several years, and I had been in my own desert experience, out of ministry after blowing up my life three years earlier. I call 2008 the year that two orphans found each other. No one was really interested in me, and the Discovery position was not high on the list of many potential pastors either. In my first week as the pastor, I was informed by the search committee that they had not told the church about my affair. That's fun! They thought it would be better that they hear that from me. I bet! Despite my shock and disappointment, I knew that we had to do it and soon. So in my fifth week as the new pastor, I preached a sermon on Peter's restoration by Jesus in John 21 and told my story. Two families left the church that day, and about half the church left over the next two months. There was so much pain in that.

The passage of time, confession, true repentance, years of counseling, healing, redemption, restoration, reconciliation, the love and support of my wife and daughters—none of that seemed to matter. Why not? The people who left the church were not bad people. They were good people who also happened to be "truth" people. The rest, the people who stayed—and a handful of them are still with us today and are real heroes of mine—rallied around this idea that we are all people with stories and that all of our stories contain some really jacked-up parts. Their hearts broke for Stacy, my girls, and me and for all that we had been through. Something happened that day through their hugs and tears. Not only did they show us Jesus, but their unconditional love and grace paved the way for us becoming the safe grace-and-truth place that we are today. Those fifty or so people who stayed modeled Jesus and what we value most in this place—full-throttle grace and full-on truth.

It's Time to Be Different

It is much easier to choose sides or to come up with a formula that we are comfortable with. That's what most of us Christians do. Grace and truth—uncompromising truth (full of truth) and unlimited grace (full of grace)—are the targets for all of us as we truly experience Jesus and try our best to follow him. Let's walk as Jesus walked, in the tension that he walked—not either-or but both-and. Let's continue to be an uncommon people of rescue who are absolutely 100 percent full of grace and absolutely 100 percent full of truth. It should be a part of who we naturally become as we continue to experience Jesus in our lives and stories.

Maybe a place to start is to remind ourselves of this. As kingdom-of-God people, we are called to love all people unconditionally, even our enemies, even people who are of a different denomination, race, social status, sexual orientation or preference, and even people who sin differently or take different political positions than we do, just as Christ did (Luke 6:27, 35). We are even commanded to use our kingdom authority to pray sincerely for those who persecute us—again, just as Christ did (Matt. 5:43–44; Luke 6:28). Pastor Greg Boyd said it this way: "Whatever our own opinions about how the kingdom of the world should run, whatever political or ethical views we may happen to embrace, our one task as kingdom-of-God disciples is to fight for people, and the way we do it is by doing exactly what Jesus did."[2] There it is again. If we say we believe in Jesus, we must walk as he walked (1 John 2:6).

As we experience Jesus, one of the biggest differences about us should be in how we respond to people who are different from us. Preston Sprinkle said that "embodying God's kindness is an essential part of Christian discipleship, especially toward those the church has shamed and shunned."[3] My seminary professor Dr. Dan Lowery once said to me, "It is always more important in disciple-making to be kind than it is to be right." When it comes to where we find ourselves as Christians and how we respond on issues of race, sexuality, and politics, something simply has to change. As Christians, when the voice that says "Yeah, but ..." starts to rise up in us, we need to get back to this. Whoever it is, whatever it is that they are choosing or deciding to do, they are made in the image of God just like you and me. God really loves them as much as he loves you and me, and so should we. Experiencing Jesus means, above all else, we should always lead with that.

Part Three

Live to Rescue

~ 9 ~

Embracing Unconventional You

"Beer is proof God loves us."

Anonymous

—◆—

Last year I took a trip to the Ivory Coast of Africa with my good friend and mentor Roy Moran. Harry Brown, president of a ministry called New Generations, also accompanied our group on the trip. I really enjoyed my time with Harry. I learned a lot from him during our conversations on those long rides on a small bus to several remote villages. What I enjoyed the most, though, is that he shares my passion for this idea that something has to change.

On one of those buses, Harry described our paradigm problem in the American church: Christians believe that ministry is not everyone's responsibility but is reserved for paid professionals. I immediately resonated with what he was saying. Not only have I witnessed that point of view, I also spent the first forty years or so of my life believing it and feeling it. I don't know that anything is keeping the church from being what Jesus always intended for it to be more than that. Somehow, someway, we have got to change that.

Even when we can move past that conclusion about ministry and embrace it as our job, we quickly find ourselves face to face with a second major challenge. We believe we are not qualified to do it. Meanwhile, a kingdom explosion is happening in Africa because ordinary people are refusing to believe that. A big part of the solution to this problem is learning how to embrace our *unconventional self.* It has taken me decades to get this, but I promise you, this is life-changing stuff. If you still feel like something is missing in your life, my question is this: Have you learned to embrace unconventional you?

This past summer I was with our staff team at a ranch in the mountains of Colorado where we hold our annual retreat. Unlike some other churches, we don't talk much about mission and strategy stuff at our retreats. We choose to do that on-site at our monthly meetings and save our retreat time for heart work and investing in each other, chasing after deeper relationships with God and with each other.

Last year at the retreat, it was finally my turn in the hot seat, time for four or five team members to download some truth from the Father into me. So, I shared where life had me, the group prayed for me, and then we sat in silence for a minute or two as they listened, wrote notes, and reflected. After a couple of minutes, Becca, DCC's children's director, said, "So I will have more to say in a minute, but I need to start with this: Greg, you are a freak, an absolute freak, a Jesus freak." I thought my heart was going to jump out of my chest. I loved it, totally and completely loved it. If that were the only thing said to me that day, I would have been good, so good. A few weeks later, Becca gave me a Nike shirt that just says "Freak" on it. I wear it with pride.

Ten years ago, five years ago even, that would have landed in a completely different way for me. It would have pressed into my insecurity and left me uncomfortable and wondering. It would have reignited my "something to prove." It landing in the way that it did last summer—as a source of joy, laughter, and affirmation, it making my heart come alive—is evidence of me experiencing and continuing to experience the healing of Jesus in my life and story, walking in sonship, and having nothing to prove. More than that, it is evidence of me learning to embrace unconventional me. This is such a critical piece of each of us becoming all that we have been uniquely created by God to be.

Different Is Good

Over the past few years, I have developed a fascination with, and love for, the word *unconventional*. That fascination was ignited by two friends. I was having coffee in town with a pastor friend named Daniel, who is lead pastor of a great church here in the Springs. Toward the end of our conversation, he said, "You are so unconventional. In fact, that should be the title of your first book." I had never really thought of that word in the context of my ministry, life, or story, and at that time, I had no plans for a book. But there was something about what he said that appealed to me.

About a year later, I was having a beer with a good buddy before he shipped out to Waco, Texas. Jerod, a.k.a. "Jrod," was Army Special Forces (SF), a Green Beret, who at that time was serving as an Army physical therapist for SF guys at Fort Carson here in the Springs. The Army was sending him to Baylor University to pursue his PhD. Jrod is an absolute stud. His wife, Kristin, a.k.a. "Kdog," is amazing too. Jrod's arms are so jacked that I like to tease him about having Kdog take in the sleeves on all his T-shirts. The dude is a warrior for the kingdom in the truest and best sense of the word and has been and continues to be a real friend.

Jrod gave me an 18 Delta SF T-shirt—18 Delta is the SF medic specialization, which is what he was when he was Special Forces. That shirt rocked my world in such a cool way. Here's why. Being a field medic is a part of our discipleship path here at DCC. We raise up people who are medics regardless of the field they work in, people who help stop the bleeding in others and get them to the help they need. That T-shirt is my favorite to this day. On the front, it says "Unconventional Warfare, Unconventional Medicine." That shirt and my friendship with Jrod further ignited the significance of this word *unconventional* in me. It helps me embrace the unconventional pastor that God created when he created me. Having said that, it has been quite the journey to get here.

Because of my law background, graduating from law school and being licensed to practice in two states, one of the questions I had early on in my transition to ministry was what kind of education or degree would be required for me to do what I was asked to do. I began to look into seminary and was so disappointed by what I discovered. My Juris Doctor (law degree) was a three-year, ninety-hour graduate degree. My research suggested that, in order to be a senior or lead pastor, I would need an MDiv, another ninety-hour graduate degree. The thought of that made me want to puke. I started taking a few classes to work in that direction, but I still don't have an MDiv. I have two master's degrees, one in ministry and one in contextual leadership, but no MDiv. Some have suggested that my lack of an MDiv makes me unqualified to do what I do. I am sure that others have mentally disqualified me for other reasons. As I moved toward ministry, I found myself in unconventional space, just one more way that I am somewhat of a "freak."

For years, I felt both unqualified and underqualified to do what God asked me to do. My story of crashing and burning in my first attempt at ministry, the strong opinions of pastors and Christians about that, my lack of the "proper" credentialing, my bad experiences with other pastors—all of it, for a long time, caused me to feel unqualified. A big part of my journey has been seeing how my journey has uniquely qualified me. A big part of my walk with God has been him teaching me to accept and embrace the beauty of unconventional me. I am hoping that this chapter puts you on that path too.

My friend Morgan Snyder, in his book *Becoming a King*, said, "The only one that underestimates your life is you."[1] I believe that, when it comes to church, Christians, and kingdom assignments, this is especially true. We need to change that. We, the church, have been sending the wrong message to our tribes for some time now. Our attempts to limit who can actually do ministry, the limitations that we place on women, the educational requirements, the lines we draw between clergy and laity and between sacred and secular are not only limiting the kingdom impact of the American church, they are keeping Christians from experiencing all the life Jesus came to bring them. That life will never be experienced outside of the third circle, without this live-to-rescue piece.

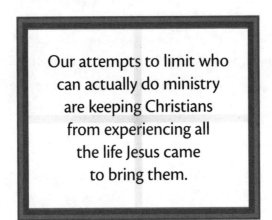

Our attempts to limit who can actually do ministry are keeping Christians from experiencing all the life Jesus came to bring them.

A. W. Tozer once said, "It is not what a man does that determines whether his work is sacred or secular, it is why he does it. The motive is everything. Let a man sanctify the Lord God in his heart and he can thereafter do no common act."[2] It is not what you do vocationally that determines whether your work is sacred or secular. What if everything that we do is a kingdom assignment and has real kingdom potential? A big part of my own journey was Jesus teaching me how to embrace the unconventional path I had followed, a path that doesn't disqualify me but instead uniquely qualifies me to make a difference in the lives of people in the world around me.

Some things in our past keep us from the life that Jesus came to bring us. But there is also unrealized and untapped kingdom potential in our past. It would be easy to write it off as irrelevant, sideways energy, or a waste of time. A better way to see it is that God was shaping and constructing unconventional me. The same is true of you.

In the past five years, I have started to understand how my past experiences are converging to help me become all that God created me to be. If not a career, what was that short Marine Corps stint all about? For the past fifteen years, I have lived and done ministry in one of the most military cities in the country—home to the United States Air Force Academy, two Air Force bases, and a major Army installation. My past experiences help me connect and relate. What about my love for the Smoky Mountains? For the past fifteen years, I have lived at the base of Pikes Peak with a view of "real" mountains every day. What about that trial-attorney thing? I honestly don't know that there could be better training for ministry. I can't help but think about what Stephen Mansfield said about Martin Luther: "For Luther beer flowed best in a vibrant Christian life. The tavern was where he learned of the world, he was called to reform with the gospel of Christ."[3] As a trial attorney, I regularly spent my time in the middle of someone else's mess, problem, or controversy. I got to swim every day in the reality of humanity and the challenges that we all face. I also got the opportunity to stand in front of the jury during a trial, people who, for the most part, didn't want to be there. My guess is that most pastors reading this can connect with that statement. Think about the people that you speak to or should be speaking to each week. As an attorney, you can't have a conversation with a jury member; it would result in an immediate mistrial. Instead, you have to read what they are thinking and then present your case so that it appeals to them and hopefully leads them to the conclusion you want them to reach. I don't know that there could be any better preparation for what I do today. Every day and every week I get to lead people on a journey that hopefully always lands in the same place: the only verdict and answer is Jesus.

Thinking about Your Past Differently

Mark Batterson said it this way: "The lions and bears in each of our lives look different, but God is getting us ready to face giants. Everything in your past is preparation for something in your future. It's the Goliath in front of us that helps us discover the David within us."[4] I love that. Everything in your past is preparation for something in your future. Everything? Yes, everything—the good, the bad, and the ugly. What if we really began to embrace that? What if we began to live every single day of our lives as if it were true?

The Apple television commercial from years back is especially appropriate here:

> Here's to the crazy ones. The misfits. The rebels. The troublemakers. The round pegs in the square holes. The ones who see things differently. They're not fond of rules. And they have no respect for the status quo. You can quote them, disagree with them, glorify or vilify them. About the only thing you can't do is ignore them. Because they change things. They push the human race forward. While some may see them as the crazy ones, we see genius. Because the people who are crazy enough to think they can change the world, are the ones who do.

I love that! The unconventional people who are crazy enough to think that they can change the world are ultimately the ones who do. Jesus believes that too. Your unconventional path is unique. Your story is too. You have been uniquely created to bring the unique kingdom difference to the world around you that you and only you can bring. God didn't walk you down that path and through that stuff, that mess, just for you. He did that to give you the ability to turn to someone else and say, "I get it. I've been there. I'm here for you." He did that to allow you to be a part of someone else's rescue.

Martin Luther King Jr. once said, "Use me, God. Show me how to take who I am, who I want to be, and what I can do, and use it for a purpose greater than myself."[5] What if that became our daily prayer? I want to challenge you to continue to become all that God has created you to be, and not to wait. Go ahead and embrace unconventional you, and watch what God does in and through your life. Just start moving toward and into the opportunities that God places in front of you. Make no mistake about it. You are qualified. If you have signed up to follow Jesus, it is your job, your calling, your mission. This "living to rescue" thing is not for the paid professionals; it's for us, all of us, each and every one of us. So, no more excuses. Start embracing unconventional you, and watch what God begins to do for, in, and through you.

— 10 —

Finding Tonto

*"Two are better than one, because they have a
good return for their labor: If either of them
falls down, one can help the other up."*

Ecclesiastes 4:9–10

———◆———

Finding the abundant life Jesus came to bring requires us to find
a Tonto. Tonto was a character in *The Lone Ranger* television series
that originally aired about seventy-five years ago. A group of six
Texas Rangers were ambushed, shot, and left for dead. Only one of
them was able to crawl to a pool of cool water, which saved his life.
This lone ranger was discovered by a Native American named Tonto.
Tonto buried the five other rangers, one of whom was the survivor's
brother, and tended to the survivor's health. At the surviving ranger's

request, Tonto made him a mask from his brother's clothes and dug an empty sixth grave, so that it would appear that he had been killed too. The lone ranger then put on the black mask and traveled with Tonto throughout the American West to assist others with the challenges they faced.

Despite the name of the series being *The Lone Ranger*, the masked man was far from alone. He had Tonto by his side at all times. On our quest to discover and stay in our own stories, to experience all that Jesus came to do for us, and to live to rescue others, we must embrace the significance of Tonto. But we often fail to do so.

Lone Wolves Die

About five years ago, before COVID, a few of us on our DCC staff team went to visit Crossroads Church in Cincinnati, Ohio. One of the big takeaways from the trip was their manifesto, which we adopted with their permission and made our own. One of the pages is titled "Lone Wolves Die." It says:

> Our society is filled with stories of individuals. Great-sounding, epic tales that actually mask insecurity and fear. Know what happens to lone wolves? They die. And die alone. Everybody needs a wolf pack. We weren't designed to do life alone. Opening up and being vulnerable is intimidating, but that bravery leads to some of the best things in life.

Every time I think about lone wolves dying, I am reminded of one of our DCC men's retreats years ago. After teaching a session, I received a text message from a man attending the retreat, whom I'll call Chuck. Chuck sent me a John Eldredge quote: "The enemy fears you. You are dangerous big-time. If you ever really get your heart back and live from it with courage, you would be a huge problem for him. You would do a lot of damage ... on the side of good."[1] Chuck went on to say, "Keep up the good work. You're killing it here. These guys are listening and responding to your words." That fired me up. God really used Chuck at that moment in my life.

Chuck was surrounded by good men at that retreat. The guys in the foxhole with him were studs, men who were committed to fighting for their hearts and helping others do the same. Chuck had an amazing wife who loved him deeply. He was her knight in shining armor. He also had a college-age daughter and a young son who looked up to him. Nevertheless, just a few years later, Chuck left his wife for another woman. Since then, he's remarried once or twice, been with several women, had multiple jobs, and moved from state to state, all in pursuit of the life his heart was desperate for.

Listen, there is absolutely no judgment here. I don't do that. People who live in glass houses like mine shouldn't throw stones, and I don't. There's no judgment, but there is sadness. It broke my heart. Chuck has huge kingdom potential. His story didn't have to read that way. He had good men, great men, surrounding him, but when the dust settled, it became clear that he kept them at arm's length. What he needed most was all around him, but behind the curtain of his life, he was a lone wolf.

What happens to lone wolves? They eventually die. I've seen it in my own story and in the lives of so many others. It took me a long, long time to apply this to my own life and story. Finding Tonto is challenging. Finding Tonto in a church setting can feel next to impossible.

The Church Dilemma

I am not judging Chuck for keeping the men around him at a distance. First, to some extent, it is our nature. Second, that is what I did for a long time with church guys too.

My own church and Christian school experience convinced me that the life I wanted would never be found in the church. Eventually, I bumped into a few guys who challenged my thinking on that. One was Rick, who was a youth pastor in another church. He drove a blue Camaro with Cragar SS wheels and a Hurst shifter, had a pretty girlfriend, seemed normal, was a pretty cool and fun guy, and loved basketball. Then there was Terry, a friend, mentor, and youth pastor in my teenage years who had played professional baseball with the Detroit Tigers and was a man's man. Gordy and Jim were two others. They dated Stacy's sisters, and we were buddies who ultimately became brothers-in-law. They too were real friends and the real deal. Last, there was Bob Russell, the man who led Southeast Christian Church in Louisville for over forty years and became my pastor when I was sixteen years old. I was a part of Southeast for over twenty years. I am so grateful for and proud of my Southeast Christian Church heritage. It has been and continues to be an amazing church doing mind-blowing things for the kingdom under my friend Kyle Idleman's leadership. I could write a chapter or two about the impact Bob Russell has had on my life over the past four-plus decades. I would have never been in ministry, doing what God created me to do, without Bob's belief and investment in me. Even when I crashed, while angry, upset, disappointed, and silent for a while, he never gave up on me. I love the man. I have never been around a leader more gifted than Bob.

Despite my love and respect for these men, I believed they were unicorns—the exceptions, not the rule—and set out to find the life I was looking for outside of the church.

I have always placed a high value on real friendships. I have always loved being a part of a team. In fact, as much as I love golf, I much prefer to play in a golf scramble. Why? Because I love being on a team. Relationships have always been important to me as well, but for decades, my best relationships, outside of my relationships with Stacy and the men I have already described, were with men outside of the church. My buddy Dave, better known as "Elvis," would become the first real exception to that.

I met Elvis when I was invited to try out for the traveling softball team at our church in Louisville. We played side by side in the outfield on that team for years. Proverbs 18:24 says, "There is a friend who sticks closer than a brother." Elvis was that. He quickly became the brother I never had. While he was serious about his faith, he never led with that. He didn't really talk about it; he lived it. He too was a graduate of the University of Louisville, and we shared a passion for the Cardinals. He was a gifted athlete himself and now has three sons and a slew of grandsons who are crazy athletic too. Elvis was also a complete goofball who was known for doing the Elvis leg shake after getting on base.

Because our team traveled and played over a hundred games a season, Elvis and I spent a lot of time together. When we weren't playing, he would often come over to sit out on the deck and talk. We eventually made a sport of it. We called it DDS (drunken deck sitting). Relax, we didn't get drunk (usually), but we did enjoy a cold beer or two and talk about the challenges of life. Elvis's friendship was a real gift to me. When I drifted in life, as I sadly often did, he never Bible-slapped me. That wasn't his style. He always guided me back in his own special way.

Through the years, despite the busyness of life and both of us being pulled in different directions, our friendship never changed for thirty-two years. In 2017, Elvis lost his battle with liver cancer. Tag-teaming his funeral and paying tribute to him alongside my pastor, mentor, and friend Bob Russell was extremely special for me. To this day, I miss Elvis a lot. I still have his old phone number in my favorites on my cell phone. I don't know who, if anyone, now has that number; I never call it. It's just a constant reminder for me of the difference that he made in my life.

That really was the first time in my life that I had ever risked a real relationship with a church guy. Most of the rest of my relationships didn't look like that. Just a few years into practicing law, Stacy's and my marriage was not in a good place. We had two young daughters, Stacy was crazy busy as a manager at UPS, and I was busy trying to make a name for myself as an attorney. After a long week in the courtroom, you could find me at Friday happy hour with my fellow prosecutor buddies rather than where I should have been, at home with my wife and our young kids. I still have a lot of regrets about many of the decisions I made and things I did during that season of my life. Like other seasons, it reminds me of the depth of God's grace and the extent to which he has rescued me.

Stacy and I ended up separating during that season. More specifically, I moved out. She never wanted that. I ended up sharing a three-bedroom apartment with an attorney buddy named Chris. Chris wasn't really a church guy at that time but was a really good man. We set up the third bedroom for my two girls, who stayed with me every other night and every other weekend.

A few months later, I was miserable and snuck into a Saturday-night church service. It was a large megachurch, and on Saturday night I was unlikely to see someone I knew. After checking in the girls, I found a seat. Bob Russell, my pastor, began to preach on spiritual leadership and church leadership. I started to cry. Deep inside, I knew that I had drifted so far from the plan that God had for my life. The next week, driving back from a court appearance in another county, I had an emotional breakdown. I felt like God was saying, "Greg, what are you doing? This is not the plan for your life. You have drifted so far away from it. This is not who you are. This is not who you want to be for Stacy and your girls. You are not the husband, father, or man that you want to be." It hit me hard, and I was crying so hard that I had to pull over to the side of the highway. I picked up the phone and called a guy named Mike.

Mike was also on that traveling softball team with Elvis and me, but I had not spoken to him in a few years. Mike was always the guy, though, who was serious and gung-ho about his faith. In the past, he had constantly invited me to Bible studies that he was leading with other men. His relentless invites agitated me and got under my skin. Still, at that moment, I knew I needed to call him. Mike rearranged his calendar and met me an hour or so later for lunch. Despite my initial hesitancy, I didn't pull any punches. I knew I was on a bad path and needed help. I told Mike the whole story.

After patiently listening to me for nearly two hours, Mike said something I will never forget: "Greg, you need some Christian men in your life. You have all these people that you are running with, but none of them really share your faith. None of them really value what you say you value. None of them are really chasing the life you say you want." He invited me to meet with a group of guys that Friday morning at 5:30 a.m. I remember thinking, *Are you kidding? 5:30? Who really does that?* I told him that I would only come if he first called the other five men and they were all good with it. He called back about an hour later and said they wanted me to come. Even after all that, I had no intention of going. Kumbaya was not my thing. It still isn't.

God had a different plan. That Friday morning, I woke up at 4:00 a.m. and couldn't go back to sleep. So, I headed out to meet Mike. The group gathered in the basement of a guy named Robert. When I walked in, Robert was in the kitchen. I immediately liked him. Eventually, the other five guys showed up, and we made our way to the basement. Mike introduced me, and the guys seemed glad I was there. I remember thinking, *These guys are all right.* That was until they said, "Okay, time to pray." Then the guys on each side of me grabbed my hands. I thought I was going to jump out of my skin. *Are you kidding me? This is not who I am or what I do. I don't hold hands with other dudes.* Despite wanting to run out of the house and never return, I felt God settle my heart. Despite my discomfort, I knew I was exactly where I needed to be.

I started showing up every Friday. A few months later, we drew straws for accountability partners, and Robert and I got paired up. He and his wife, Tracy, had two young daughters, the same ages as Stacy's and mine. Besides that, we could not have been more different. He was so freaking funny, loved to goof off, and made me laugh often and hard. I could not have taken life and myself more seriously. One of Stacy's favorite memories is of me on the phone with Robert, laughing so hard I could hardly catch my breath. Something started to change in my life. I remember thinking, *Maybe I can really be friends with a few Christian men after all.*

Shortly after joining the group, Robert plugged me into a good counselor he had seen, and I moved back home to start working on being the husband, father, and man I wanted to be. Robert and I held each other accountable. Unfortunately, we had no context or category for the story piece discussed in the first four chapters of this book. I remain sad about that. But my relationship with him helped me become a better man, husband, and father to my girls. He walked with me, encouraged me, and challenged me when I desperately needed it.

Tragically, Robert was killed in a traffic accident just a few years later. I found his car abandoned on the highway, and the police officer on the scene told me what had happened. I raced to his house. The six of us guys stood in his driveway most of that night, while our wives were in the house caring for Tracy, his wife. Being there while she explained to their two young daughters when they woke up the next morning that Daddy was gone was brutal. I will never forget it. It was one of the saddest moments of my life.

To this day, twenty-six years later now, I still think of Robert. He, like Elvis, made a real difference in my life. He was another Tonto, a guy whose friendship helped convince me that real relationships with other Christians might be beneficial after all. I started to be open to that, and in some ways, I started to pursue it. We all need a Tonto or two in our lives. There is nothing like having a few people who are chasing God in a similar way, people who challenge you, spend time with you, encourage you, hold you accountable, and believe in you. All of that is great, but the real gold is found in one last missing piece—a piece that I would not discover or understand until about ten years later, when I was on the backside of a significant, embarrassing, horrific, public moral failure.

People Who Know Your Story and Believe in You

I've already described a few of the special, life-changing moments I had in my eight years with my mentor Craig. There were so many more. If I took a journey back through my journals, I would see enough moments there to complete another book. Maybe someday that will happen. No person has ever taught me more about life with God than Craig did—no one.

A few years into our friendship and journey together, I found myself talking to Craig about the men who were up-and-coming leaders in our church. We were now a few years into doing life together, and I was talking with him about our first two-night retreat that was coming up. Craig asked me what we were going to do at the retreat. I explained that I was going to cast a vision for where we were headed as a church, that I had some Andy Stanley stuff I wanted to share, a couple of videos cued up to watch, and a PowerPoint laying out this new cutting-edge strategy for the church. The more I talked, the more excited I got about our time together. When I got to the end, Craig just looked at me and said something like, "Okay then." I was like, "What do you mean 'okay then'? That's great stuff." He said, "Yeah, it's just not what I would do." I was pissed. I didn't want to, but I asked him what he would do. He said, "I would take turns allowing each man to tell the rest of you his story, then pray for and over that man, and then allow the next man to do the same thing." I said, "That's it?" He said, "That's it."

I was less than enthused and unconvinced. That was obviously no way to grow a freaking church, and remember, I had something to prove. We were a struggling church at a critical juncture in a city that was full of churches. More of the same was not going to work. We were dying a slow death. We needed to talk about strategy. We had to talk about change. Despite everything inside of me saying "no, no, no," I'm still not sure how or why, but I scrapped my plan and went with Craig's instead. We spent about an hour total on vision and strategy and the remaining part of our two-plus days telling our personal stories and praying over and for each other. That was one of the greatest leadership decisions I have made in my entire life. Those guys were ordained as our first elders about a year and a half later. We left that time together relationally and spiritually connected at a level I didn't know or think was possible. It blew my mind.

The Beatles sing about us getting by with a little help from our friends. It's true. Some of us also get high with a little help from our friends, as they also sing. As I have said, there is nothing like having a few people in your life who are chasing God in a similar way, people who challenge you, spend time with you, encourage you, hold you accountable, and believe in you. Even better is having people who really and truly know your story and still believe in you. Do you have that in your life? Don't you want that in your life? Trust me, you do, you really do. We all need to find a Tonto or two in our lives. We tend to think the test of our spiritual maturity is what we know or how much we know. It's not. As Craig said, "One of the greatest indicators of spiritual maturity is the quality of our closest relationships." What if we simply began to live every day of our lives as if that were true?

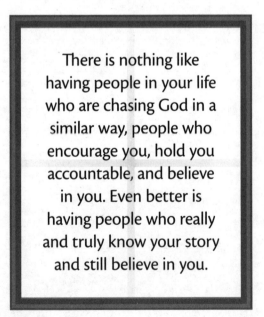

There is nothing like having people in your life who are chasing God in a similar way, people who encourage you, hold you accountable, and believe in you. Even better is having people who really and truly know your story and still believe in you.

Who Is in the Foxhole with You?

I am grateful for Craig and his influence in my life for a lot of reasons. I am especially grateful for him giving me the key to what real relationships in Jesus with people around us can really be. For the first forty-three years of my life, I missed out on the depth of relationship that I have begun to experience in the last fifteen years. Because of my focus on real relationships, built on and based on story, there are a few more Elvises, Roberts, and Craigs in my life. I don't know where I would be without Bob, Jon, Yemi, Morgan, Kevin, Reed, John, Terry, Warren, and Jud. There are a few special ladies, including Pastor MJ and Tamara, my assistant, who are also Tontos to the extent that they can and should be in my life and story too.

There are so many more stories I could tell of the impact of others in my life as they have done life in the foxhole with me. I just want to take time for one more.

A few days after Craig passed away in 2016, I went over to the Wild at Heart Outpost to meet with Morgan. In that conversation, he said something to me that I will never forget. He said, "Buddy, you know that Craig's ministry mantle is not being handed to me; it's being handed to you." I remember thinking, *Wow, who in this world really does that?* Morgan had been on the team with Craig and spent much more time with him over the years than I had. It would be natural for him to want, expect, and accept that mantle. Instead, he bestowed it on me. That moment touched me deeply and connected our hearts in an unbelievable way. I am so grateful for that and the way that Morgan continues to invest in my life.

There are still others. Each of our church staff team is in the foxhole every day beside me. I love them all deeply. Even when I can't see it, they are close enough to see and speak into all that God himself has created me, Greg Lindsey, to be. If you haven't experienced that, I promise you it's available. You really need to experience it. Take a chance. Start pursuing a few real Tonto relationships in your life. Lone wolves simply die. Lone Christian wolves do too.

I want to go back to when my Special Forces buddy Jrod gave me my treasured 18 Delta T-shirt before he moved on to Waco. That same day, he also gave me a 10th Group SF Challenge Coin and the SF (Green Berets) insignia pin. The pin has the SF motto on it: "De Oppresso Liber," which is Latin for "To free the oppressed." To me, that sounds a lot like Jesus' mission, the one he handed to us. That motto is another way to express my own heart and passion: to live to rescue others. I have that insignia pin stuck through the front cover of my leather journal. I see it every morning and keep the challenge coin in my coin rack on my desk. I love that insignia so much that I even bought a large one that hangs on the wall beside the window in my home office. I'm looking at it as I type this. More than any of that, though, what meant the most to me was what Jrod wrote in his note to me. I keep it tucked inside my journal. He called me an unconventional pastor, he called me the number-one force multiplier he knows, he spoke to my glory. He knows my story and believes in me.

There is nothing quite like empowering words from someone who is in the foxhole with us. We all need a Tonto or two in our lives. Who is yours? Are you confident of the heart, mind, and dialogue of the person, or those few people, who are hunkered down in the foxhole with you? If not, stay on the quest to find a Tonto or two in your life. It is an indispensable part of you finding the life you are looking for, an indispensable part of you becoming all that you were created to be. Yes, live to rescue, live to rescue everyone that you can, everyone that you know, every day of your life, but never ever attempt to do it alone.

A Call to Action with a Sense of Urgency

*"Every Christian is either a
missionary or an imposter."*

Charles Spurgeon

❖

That Spurgeon quote doesn't sit well with me. I mean, what was he drinking when he came up with that? For the vast majority of my life, I haven't felt like either of those things. It feels offensive. If you are feeling that, I get it. I'm not suggesting it's without merit. I am suggesting that we spend just a little bit of time wrestling with it. About six years ago, our mission statement at DCC was to help people discover their story, experience Jesus, and live on mission. We were in a sermon series on our mission, and I was preparing a sermon on the phrase "live on mission." As I sat there staring at those three words and the blinking cursor on the screen in front of me, the words felt off, generic, over-cooked, overused, and empty.

I wrote out the three words on the yellow legal pad in front of me. (Having spent ten years as a trial attorney, that is still how I prepare. Old habits die hard.) After a few more minutes of staring at them, I crossed them out and wrote "live to rescue" beside them. I felt something starting to stir in me. I thought, *That's it! That's the missing piece. That is what it is supposed to be. That is who we are.* It was actually who we had been for the past ten years, who God was really asking us to be. "Live to rescue" had a sense of urgency that "live on mission" didn't have. "Live to rescue" said something significant was happening and at stake. It said that I needed to do something. It was a call to action with a sense of urgency, suggesting that if I didn't do something, something bad might happen. The passion that was ignited in me that day has never faded. The more I thought about it, prayed about it, talked with our elders and a few others about it, the more it became clear. Just a few months later, we changed our DCC mission statement: We exist to help people discover their stories, experience Jesus, and live to rescue.

We also changed our church logo to a red, distressed, grunge cross on a white circle background inside of a square. Think of the American Red Cross logo with enough alterations to stay clear of copyright issues. As a former attorney, I didn't want to deal with the hassle of being sued. You can look up our logo if you are interested. It remains the same today. We've often thought that if we would change the cross on the sign on our building from red to green, we would attract a lot more people. It is Colorado.

A Lifestyle of Sacrifice

Let me explain the real why behind the change. The red cross on a white background is what one typically sees on an ambulance, hospital, or even the helmet of a combat medic. My understanding is that the logo originated about 160 years ago in Italy, when a Swiss man witnessed forty thousand wounded soldiers suffering and dying on a battlefield. He began to organize local people to help the wounded and dying soldiers. They identified themselves with this symbol. Ordinary people helping people. The symbol was then adopted by the Geneva Convention in 1864 as a symbol of an organization that would offer help to all.

While our logo is similar to the Red Cross logo, the vertical beam on the cross in our logo is a little longer, more consistent with the Roman cross that Jesus was crucified on. One of the hills we die on (our core values) at DCC is "Die to Self." As you might expect, it is not our most popular core value. But the abundant life we are all looking for requires it. I love former Navy SEAL Medic Mark Donald's definition of *warrior*: "One who chooses a lifestyle of personal sacrifice." The cross logo reminds us of that lifestyle choice. It's a cross to remind us that Jesus came to rescue us and that he asks us to take up our own cross daily, following him wherever he leads and being about his business of rescuing others. To honor and respect the distinction of those who wear the red cross in a white circle faithfully and courageously every single day, ours is contained in a square. The faded, grunge, distressed, worn-out look points to the realities of the battles and mess we face in life and to the messiness of a life committed to helping bring rescue, help, and hope.

People tend to move toward images like this one in hopes of receiving the help and rescue that they need. However, most people have given up on church being that kind of place. Our passion at DCC is changing that point of view one heart, life, story, and person at a time.

Finding a Tonto or two in your life is not enough. You need more than just a few of the right people to do life with. You need a few of the right people who are also united around a common mission. I heard John Eldredge say that several years ago, and it immediately rocked me. It has since changed my life. Without a common mission, the relationships often eventually fade or fizzle out. I have seen that time and time again in my life. It is true inside and outside the church. There is such tremendous life-giving power in relationships that are centered on this call to action with a sense of urgency that God has on our lives.

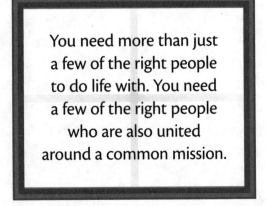

You need more than just a few of the right people to do life with. You need a few of the right people who are also united around a common mission.

If I had written this chapter a few years ago, it would have been totally different. I have since learned a lot about what God intended for the Christian life and his church to be. God has been lovingly, intentionally, and fiercely disrupting me for some time now. In short, if I had written this back then, I would have told you that your call to action is to come to church and become a great inviter. Invite everyone that you know to come and see, become an usher, serve in the church, invite and invest in the church. Years ago, that phrase, "come and see," had been adopted as a core value by a huge church we are big fans of and have a relationship with. So, we adopted it too. There is even a sermon out there somewhere in cyberspace called "Come and See" by yours truly. Five years ago, we were in the one hundred fastest-growing churches in America for a few years running. We were riding "come and see" hard, really hard, and everything was up and to the right (growth curve) for us. We were riding the wave that many others were riding, the wave of the church-growth season. That's when God began to really disrupt me.

Over the past six years or so God has shown me that the church should be less about "come and see" and more about "come and go"—a place to come and then go and be who God created you to be. Church should be a place where we are challenged, encouraged, charged up, and sent out to be all that God meant for us to be. I could say so much more about this, but for now, church is not the building; we are the church. There are no exceptions to that. This call to action, with a sense of urgency, is for all of us. It is a call beyond showing up, giving, serving, and inviting others to church. For a long time, I missed that.

At the end of 2017, I was preaching on a Saturday night one weekend in November and immediately realized that the crowd was unusually large. When the weekend numbers came in, we were about thirty-five people short of breaking three thousand in attendance on a non-holiday weekend for the first time. I remember thinking, *Yes!!!!* and wishing someone was there for me to fist-bump or high-five in that moment. *Oh, yeah, more up and to the right. Booyah, naysayers. There you go. Take that. Let's go, baby. Four thousand, watch out, because you're next. Here we come.* That lasted for about twenty seconds. That's when my joy and celebration turned to a sense of panic. My thought was, *Three thousand what?* With all due respect to everyone who was there that weekend, the answer that came to mind was, *Three thousand mostly spectators and consumers.* I remember thinking that we had to challenge people more, disciple people more and better, teach people what it means to really take up one's cross and follow Jesus. So, we set out to do that at the beginning of 2018.

Long story short, our average weekend attendance dropped by five hundred people between 2018 and the beginning of the COVID shutdown of 2020. We actually had two shutdowns; the second time because 75 percent of our staff contracted COVID in November of that year. It was brutal. Every pastor I know has COVID stories. I just want to share one quickly with you that's relevant here.

Sometime during our reopening after the first COVID shutdown, I had a man approach me in the lobby between services. I recognized him and knew that we had spoken a few times but did not know his name. At that time, I kept a mask around my neck between services. If someone came up to me with a mask on, I would pull mine up, and if not, I would leave it down. We can argue about the approach another time. It was a no-win season for any decision on that front. Anyway, as he approached me, I had just turned from a conversation with a person wearing a mask, so my mask was still up. This man immediately pointed to my mask and said, "I don't like that." I said, "Okay." He said, "I'll tell you what. My wife and I give five hundred dollars per month to the church. If you make that go away, we'll up it to eight hundred." As he walked away, he turned and said, "You think about that." Christians! Bless their little hearts!

About six months later, I was out in the lobby after preaching, and here he came again. He had a huge smile on his face, which made me wonder what was going on. The first words out of his mouth were, "So, we're leaving your church today." I said, "Okay." He poked me in the chest with his finger and said, "You've lost your fire. You don't have the same fire you had when we started coming here, so we're leaving. We may come back to visit, but we're leaving. You need to find your fire." As he walked away, he said, "You need to care less about this city and more about this church." I haven't seen him since. Is it wrong to say that I don't really want to? I haven't seen him since, but I have thought a lot about that moment. I don't know it and can't prove it, but I think the continual challenge and constant reminders of the call to action on his life with a sense of urgency did not sit well with him. I'm convinced that my lobby buddy was not comfortable with all the change and disruption that we were trying to bring into his life. This call to action is not just for any given group of people that happens to gather on the weekend and call itself a church. As followers of Jesus, it is for each and every one of us.

Jesus Revolution Part 2

Jon Petersen is a friend and mentor of mine whom I love spending time with. His phrase "kingdom mischief" is one that I love, have stolen, and use a lot today. A few years back, he handed me a book called *From Megachurch to Multiplication: A Church's Journey toward Movement* by a pastor in Texas named Chris Galanos. When he gave it to me, he said, "I don't know, but I think there is something for and about Discovery here." Chris's book ultimately led me to three or four more books, which led me to three or four more.

I started reading all I could about what God was doing around the world through disciple-making movements. On that journey, I eventually read *Spent Matches* by my pastor friend and mentor in Kansas City, Roy Moran, who I mentioned traveling to Africa with. Roy spends the first part of the book really unpacking the hard truth, what all the research reveals, about the church in America. If research is your thing, God bless you, you will love it. The entire book is a great read on how we can begin to bring what God is doing in other parts of the world here to the American church. We need to. The kingdom is exploding in growth in other parts of the world. The numbers are staggering and amazing, despite the persecution and challenges that come in areas of the world that often have a heavy Muslim influence. Living to rescue is happening exponentially in other parts of the world, and it is not the ordained, paid ministry professionals who are doing it. In 2022 alone, New Generations tracked 14,000 new churches, 210,000-plus new disciples, and 36 new disciple-making movements. God is on the move in this world. Jesus Revolution Part 2 is stirring.

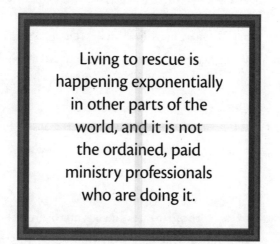

Living to rescue is happening exponentially in other parts of the world, and it is not the ordained, paid ministry professionals who are doing it.

The question is, why is that not happening here? I don't want to oversimplify it, but the bottom line is this: It is not happening here because followers of Jesus are not embracing the call to action on their individual lives and the sense of urgency around that. It is not happening because we are stuck in this thinking that it is not our job, and even if it is, we are not qualified to do it. Nothing could be further from the truth. We are making it harder than it really is. Pastor J. D. Greear is a great pastor of a great church in North Carolina. I love his definition of *discipleship*: "One person learning from another person what it means to follow Jesus." Are we making this harder than it is? When I was in Africa last year, Harry Brown, president of New Generations, had several great quotes that I wrote down. I called them Harry-isms. One of my favorites was this: "It's not the size of your fire; it's the number of fires you start." It is not the size of our church; it's the number of fires we start. The more people we have embracing the call to action to be fire starters, the more fires we are going to start. We need more fire starters. Disciple-making movements are all about making disciples who make disciples who make disciples. It is about ordinary people accepting the call to action with a sense of urgency that exists in each of their lives.

I can't speak of fire starters without talking about my friends Jeremy, Bryan, and the team at Wild Courage in Idaho, who are living out all that we are talking about in this chapter. They are simply getting men around fires with a distinct purpose of sharing stories and listening to each other's stories. There is no teaching, preaching, advice, or pressure, just permission to be who you are and share your story. The attendees are diverse—believers, nonbelievers, pastors, neighbors, friends, coworkers, you name it. All are welcome. Some share more than others. Others just sit and listen. It is simple. Pray it up, invite guys in, light the fire, and watch how God shows up. God is doing amazing things through their sense of urgency and saying yes to his call to action. There are now "fires" happening in many other states. If you want to know more, I encourage you to check them out at www.thewildcourage.life.

My second daughter, Sloane, played college basketball during her freshman year at Colorado Christian University in Denver, a Division II school. After her freshman year, she decided that if she was going to work that hard, she wanted and needed to get paid. So, she quit basketball and took a job waiting tables at Bonefish Grill, which worked out great for her. It was the right decision. Before she quit, during her freshman year, her team won the NCCAA Division I National Championship. They were a deep, mature, and very talented team, made up of mostly juniors and seniors. Sloane was learning the ropes of college basketball as a freshman and didn't play much. That may be why her national championship ring is still in the sock drawer of my dresser. There is a difference in being on the team and in the game. My question for you is this: You may be on the team, but are you in the game?

We haven't killed the weekend service at DCC. It has its place, and people continue to find a safe MASH unit where they are led to the hope, life, rescue, and freedom that is only available in Jesus. While we haven't killed it, we have definitely started to talk about it differently. We acknowledge that what we do on the weekend is important, but we are now clearer than ever that it is not what's most important. We describe it this way: the weekend experience is a great place to start and an absolutely terrible place to stop.

Life with Jesus is about so much more than what we experience on any given weekend at any given church. It is not about "come and see" but each of us being willing to "go and be" the church. We challenge people to stop sharing their faith (wait for it, don't freak out, another Christian twitch moment) and start living their faith and sharing their lives. We are clear that the live-to-rescue mission of Jesus is all about multiplication and not addition. We challenge everyone every week to leave the building and be the sent person God has created them to be. We teach them that living to rescue is being intentional about living their faith, their life with God, in all the places where they live, learn, work, and play. We challenge them to sense the urgency and step into the call on their life. I want to challenge you to do it too. All of us have been created to be in the game. There are no bench players on Team Jesus.

The Answer Is You

A big part of stepping into this is learning to let go of the pressure we feel. There is no pressure to be a scholar, teacher, pastor, or evangelist. Jesus is looking for people who are willing to come alongside and help rescue others. He's looking for people who are willing to look someone else in the eye and say, "I get it. I've been through some stuff too. Now let me help you." He's not looking for people who fix people but people who are willing to help stop the bleeding and get them to the help they really need. Jesus is looking for people who will step into the call to action that is on their lives and live to rescue others.

One final thought before we leave this. I know that this final section of the book is on living to rescue, and I am placing a lot of emphasis on that. It's important, but as you set out to step into it and do it, make sure you don't miss this: remember where we started. All three circles all the time. What I am pointing to specifically is the story piece. My experience has been this. We often have our Jesus experience and then get busy for Jesus. There's nothing wrong with that. It is better than never having an experience with Jesus at all or living a self-centered life. Two observations, though. First, we have to overcome the tendency we have in the church and as Christians to reduce life with Jesus to a magic moment. That moment when you said yes to Jesus was magical. It changed your life forever. Or if you haven't done it, you really should. Having said that, it is so easy to reduce life to that magic moment or to other magic moments and really miss out on the miraculous movement that God is stirring up in the world and inviting each of us into.

The second observation is this. You have been rescued and are continuing to be rescued by Jesus to help rescue others. On your quest to experience Jesus more and live to rescue others, don't overlook your need to stay in your own story. The enemy's relentless assault of your heart and his attempts to use your story to take you out will not end. The good news is that there is always more hope, life, healing, restoration, and redemption available with Jesus. As you live to rescue others, don't forget about your own need for continuing rescue in your own life and story. Whenever you are at a point in your own life and story where things are hard, and you really believe you have lost your way, return to those three circles. Be honest with yourself about where you are. If you are outside of all three, like I have been at times in my life, I would encourage you to jump back into the "Experience Jesus" circle first. Start there, and begin to work your way back to the center, back to all three circles all the time, one day at a time. Regardless of where you find yourself, there is always a way back to true north. There is a call to action with a sense of urgency on all our lives. Remember, though, we best rescue others as we continue to be rescued ourselves by Jesus. Remember, we are never ever out of the fight.

I read Mark Batterson's book *In a Pit with a Lion on a Snowy Day* after my crash while I was in the desert out of ministry, and it reignited hope in me, reminded me of who God has created me to be, and forever changed my outlook and my life. He has since written *Chase the Lion*. This Lion Chaser's Manifesto comes from that book:

> Quit living as if the purpose of living is to arrive safely at death. Grab life by the mane. Set God-sized goals. Pursue God-ordained passions. Go after a dream that is destined to fail without divine intervention. Keep asking questions. Keep making mistakes. Keep seeking God. Stop pointing out problems and become part

of the solution. Stop repeating the past and start creating the future. Stop playing it safe and start taking risks. Expand your horizons. Accumulate experiences. Consider the lilies. Enjoy the journey. Find every excuse you can to celebrate everything you can. Live like today is the first day and last day of your life. Don't let what's wrong with you keep you from worshiping what's right with God. Burn sinful bridges. Blaze a new trail. Criticize by creating. Worry less about what people think and more about what God thinks. Don't try to be who you are not. Be yourself. Laugh at yourself. Quit holding out. Quit holding back. Quit running away. Chase the lion.[1]

T. S. Eliot is recorded as saying: "The greatest proof of Christianity is not how far a man can logically analyze his reasons for believing, but how far in practice he will stake his life on his belief." It's not nearly as much about how we can articulate our reasons for believing as it is about how much we will stake our lives on our beliefs. Are you willing to accept the call to action with the sense of urgency that is right in front of you today? We, you and me, are God's plan A, and guess what? There really is no plan B. There is a call to action with a sense of urgency on your life. What is one step that you can take today toward and into that?

— 12 —

A Dangerous Militia

*"God is breathing on the dry bones of this generation,
raising up the most unlikely people from the most
unpromising places and turning us, even us, into
a dangerous militia worthy of his name."*

Pete Greig

— ◇ —

A little over two years ago, I was alone at a small cabin owned by some friends near Cripple Creek, Colorado. Much of this book was written there. But on that particular day, God was only beginning to stir up the thoughts that would ultimately lead to this book, and I was simply trying to make some sense of it all. If you are still reading to this point, hopefully you think it worked. While I was there, I was occasionally texting with a few of our elders and our team back in the Springs. They were encouraging me in what God was stirring in me. While all their texts were great, one particular text stood out. It was from Pastor Haley on our staff team. It said, "You are a shepherd of misfit mustangs, a leader of those called to run." It was not by any stretch the most encouraging or complimentary thing that had ever been said about me as a leader, but like the word *freak* at staff retreat, something really resonated with me about that statement. I've often thought of and referred to our church as the "island of misfit toys," and the message seemed to connect with that and with another key part of my heart as a leader.

What I have come to realize is that I am more drawn to untraditional than traditional, to unconventional more than conventional. It is true in almost every context of my life. I am more drawn to unconventional warfare than conventional warfare. Rather than a regular conventional army, I am much more drawn to militia. When I heard the term "misfit mustangs," I immediately found myself attaching the word *militia*. When I look at what God is asking me to lead, I see it. We are the "Misfit Mustang Militia." It is what we as Christians are all being called up and into, who and what we are all being called to be.

If you find yourself trying to get an image in your mind of what I am talking about, I would encourage you to go watch or rewatch the movie *The Patriot*. Yes, it is gory, and yes, it is rated R. I know you are a Christian. You should still watch it. It is based on the true story of an officer in the Continental Army during the Revolutionary War named Francis Marion, a.k.a. "The Swamp Fox." When I think about or see the conventional warfare tactics of the Revolutionary War, I can't help but think, *How stupid is that?* Troops line up side by side in rows, facing the enemy, taking turns loading and shooting at each other. Cannonballs are taking off legs and heads. It really came down to the last man standing. In *The Patriot*, Benjamin Martin (the character based on Francis Marion), who led the militia, decided to fight differently. It was, by definition, unconventional and turned out to be what the Americans needed to win the war. A militia is a fighting force raised up from the civil population. It often includes no professional soldiers at all. They are an unconventional fighting force that usually fights unconventionally.

My fascination with unconventional warfare eventually led me to a fascinating book called *The Devil's Brigade*. It describes a specific unconventional fighting force that was put together in WWII called First Special Service Force (FSSF). The FSSF was a battalion organized in 1942 and is the predecessor to all Special Forces today. The men selected for the force were often misfits and screwups who were even selected and taken from the stockades. They were trained in parachuting, demolitions, small unit tactics, skiing, hand-to-hand combat, rock climbing, sixty-mile humps with eighty pounds on their backs, whatever it took to be ready for the mission. They were an elite force known for their toughness, a willingness to ignore the heavy odds against survival, and a refusal to quit. They are best known for taking a mountain in Italy that had become a German stronghold. Experts predicted it would take three days. They took it in two *hours*. After this fighting force accomplished the impossible, the Germans named them "The Devil's Brigade." The V-42 dagger was a knife designed exclusively for them by their commanding officer. No one else carried it in battle. I have given an engraved replica of this knife, along with a very special letter, to my sons-in-law, a few other special men in my life, and all my grandsons on their first birthdays. My third grandson, Graham (seventh grandchild), was born this morning as I was typing this. I can't wait for him to get his V-42 dagger this Christmas at eight months old. The FSSF, yet another misfit militia, made a huge difference.

A Holy Disruption

Where am I going with all of this? I agree with Pete Greig. I believe that God is trying to raise up a dangerous militia worthy of his name. I believe that Jerry Trousdale, in his book *Miraculous Movements*, has accurately unpacked God's strategy for the kingdom difference he wants to bring to the world around us. Here it is: "Ordinary People. Transformed Lives. Genuine Love. Remarkable Courage. Extraordinary Outcomes." Read through the Bible. That's God's rescue plan. It has always been his rescue plan. What could God do with someone like you? The answer is clear and simple: change the world.

A big part of our problem is that, when we think of church, we think more regular army than we do militia. We think in terms of large weekend gatherings with paid staff, clergy, or professionals leading the way. I thought this way exclusively, until God disrupted that at the end of 2017. When the COVID crisis hit the world in 2020, things began to change in the church. No judgment or condemnation, but many pastors and leaders have been trying to get the church back to what it was before. Some have even succeeded in doing that. Nothing wrong with that. It is simply more of a "regular army" way of thinking. But why would we return to something that wasn't working? I think God wants to use that disruption for something different. There is no right or wrong here, but we at DCC have decided to take a different approach. We have stayed on the path that God started leading us down at the end of 2017, a path that already led to declining weekend attendance, a path that has caused us to recover weekend attendance at a much slower pace than many churches around us. While that is true, pound for pound, we are stronger than we have ever been. God has taught us and continues to teach us to look at church differently, as more of the misfit militia that we believe he wants us to be. Trust me, there is a place in the kingdom militia for someone like you.

Jesus is going to build his church, and hell is not going to stop it. That is true of church in multiple expressions. House church can be a powerful, great thing. So can church in a brewery, workplace, or on the street. You name it. In fact, one of the most awesome expressions of church I have ever seen was the "Church Under the Tree" in Africa, which was exactly that. They didn't call themselves that; they simply met under a tree. The Holy Spirit was all over that. If you can't find a church in your city that floats your boat, start one. Grab a few friends and start some life together around a table with Jesus. The life that Stacy and I get to do around the table with nine other special people is often our best "church" experience of the week. This is not really about the church; it is more about our Christian thinking. I believe that God wants to continue to disrupt our American Christian way of thinking, to have us think not *institution* but *movement*, and to begin to see this stuff not as either-or but as both-and.

> I believe that God wants to continue to disrupt our American Christian way of thinking, to have us think not *institution* but *movement*, and to begin to see this stuff not as either-or but as both-and.

To rise up and become the dangerous militia God is calling us to be, we also have to lean hard into this: one people, one race, one family, one blood, and one united church. This past year, we did a "One United Church" series at DCC. Four pastors from four different churches did a four-week series, speaking at a different church each week. The results were phenomenal. I have had many of our DCC tribe ask when we are going to do that again. I don't know if we will get there, but the dream is to have dozens of churches in groups of four doing this in our city during a designated month every year.

Do you remember me telling about sharing my story with a group of pastors in Colorado Springs shortly after arriving there? I thought they were writing me off, and I found much joy and took great pride in proving them wrong about me. Five years later, our church had grown to over a thousand people. Around that time, I was approached by Pastor Thomas Thompson, who was now leading this group of pastors called "The Merge." He asked me to come back. I quickly told him that I couldn't do that, reminding him of what had happened five years earlier. He didn't flinch, told me to pray about it, and asked me to host a meeting. Long story short, we did that in April 2014.

During the meeting, I told the sixty or so pastors in attendance what a source of pain they had been in my life and also told them that most of that was not their fault. I asked them for forgiveness and admitted that I was not healed enough from my own pastor trauma to stand in a room full of pastors and tell my story. I then challenged them. I said, "We have to tear down the walls that we have built between us and begin to work together to show the love of Jesus to the people of our city, with no strings attached. The unchurched crowd of Colorado Springs couldn't care less if we filled up the Air Force Academy football stadium for a night of worship. How can we help meet the needs of our city?" That moment was one of a few catalyst moments that led to the creation of COSILoveYou, an organization committed to uniting and igniting the local church so that every woman, man, and child of Colorado Springs experiences the love of Jesus, with no strings attached. More than one hundred local churches are now a part of that at some level. It is an amazing movement. You can learn more at cosiloveyou.com.

All of that to say, everything changed for me when I started to think in terms of a dangerous militia. The dangerous militia that God is trying to raise up is so much bigger than any one church. I realized that our vision of redefining what people think when they hear the words *church* and *Christian* is so much bigger than us and something that we alone will never be able to accomplish. This misfit militia that God has in mind is a kingdom thing, not a church thing. Regardless of the number of campuses, number of people attending, and the size of the budget, the movement that God is dreaming of is so much bigger than any one church. It is the beauty of what the COSILoveYou movement is accomplishing. The people of our city are taking note of the difference that we are making, and no one church gets, takes, or tries to take the credit. This is just another version of dangerous militia and not regular army thinking.

One last way that we have been thinking about church differently for the past few years is when it comes to our building. We have a 65,000-square-foot renovated grocery store that looks more like an REI store than it does a church, and I love it. Last year, we recognized that it was our most underutilized resource and decided to deploy it for events, meetings, concerts, and co-op workspace, with a full-time coffee and food operator for the lobby.

We are also currently pursuing partnership with a preschool tenant to serve the serious needs of our community. I know several churches do several of these things, preschools, coffee shops, etc. We have decided to push it a little further. We have taken our church sign off the building and moved it around the corner to where the offices are located. The center marquee sign on the building reads "Cos City Hub." In addition, all church signage inside the building has been removed and replaced with digital monitors. In just a matter of minutes, the entire building can be branded for whoever is having an event there. We even have a "Hub" sign covering the auditorium cross that hangs above the stage during secular events. (I know, another Christian twitch moment.) With no real marketing at all, the Hub is beginning to meet a big need in our city, and more importantly, our tribe is getting the opportunity to interact and do some life with people who would never walk into a church. If you are interested, you can learn more at coscityhub.com. Yes, it is disrupting the Christian mindset that church is a building. We continue to have conversations about that, and we welcome that. Somehow, someway, we have to move from the institution that we have allowed ourselves to become back to the movement, the dangerous militia, that we were always intended to be.

Transformed Desperation

The goal is not being different to be different; it is being willing to be different to make a big difference in the world around us. The goal is to rise up and become the dangerous militia that God has created and called us to be. That happens one person at a time. No, it is not easy, but I can't find any promise anywhere that it is supposed to be or is going to be. My buddy, fellow misfit, author, and kingdom guy Hugh Halter said it this way: "God's mission is not for the faint of heart. The issue is understanding that avoiding the world is not necessarily the highest form of Christlikeness."[1] What's the promise? Jesus said it this way: "Whoever wants to save their life will lose it, but whoever loses their life for me will find it" (Matt. 16:25). We find the lives we have been looking for when we rise up and become the dangerous militia that God has created and called us to be.

Now, you really should hear the rest of Navy SEAL Jason Redman's story that we started in chapter 6. After overcoming his mistake while looking to prove himself, he found himself back on the SEAL teams. In 2007, while leading a mission to find and capture a key Al-Qaeda commander, his team was ambushed. Jason was shot twice in his left arm. As he turned to look at his arm, he took a bullet just beside his right ear that traveled through his face and took his nose off his face. Once he regained consciousness, he called out to God, "Please help me get home." He did get home. He would spend the next few years of his life in and out of the hospital.

While he was in the hospital, he wrote this and put it on his door:

> Attention to all who enter here. If you are coming into this room with sorrow or to feel sorry for my wounds, go elsewhere. The wounds I received, I got in a job I love, doing it for people I love, supporting the freedom of a country I deeply love. I am incredibly tough and will make a full recovery. What is full? That is the absolute utmost physically my body has the ability to recover. Then I will push that about 20% further through sheer mental tenacity. This room you are about to enter is a room full of fun, optimism, and intense rapid regrowth. If you are not prepared for that, Go Elsewhere. From The Management.[2]

That's a guy who refuses to let his circumstances limit his expectations. After thirty-seven surgeries, he had to retire as a SEAL. He spends his time today helping others rise up and overcome the challenging circumstances that they face in life. You can find out more at jasonredman.com.

One specific quote of Jason's continues to shape my life. Maybe it will help you: "The mark of a man is not found in his past, but how he overcomes adversity and builds his future. Quitting is not an option."[3]

Stay in your story, experience Jesus, and live to rescue others. Whatever you do, however your story reads, don't quit. Most of us, at times in our lives, have been dangerous. There is an opportunity in front of all of us to be dangerous for good. I want to challenge you to step up, rise up, and take your unique spot in the dangerous militia that God is raising up in the world around you. Your life and the lives of other people near you and throughout the world depend on it. I love Alan Hirsch's definition of *church*: "Contrary to many of the images of church as a defensive fortress suffering the relentless onslaughts of the enemy. The movement that Jesus set in motion is an advancing, untamed, and untamable revolutionary force created to transform the world."[4]

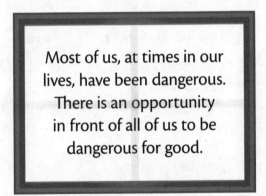

Most of us, at times in our lives, have been dangerous. There is an opportunity in front of all of us to be dangerous for good.

We will never be that collectively until we are willing to embrace and commit to who God has uniquely created each of us to be individually. Each of us becoming all that we can be is about more than setting and pursuing goals; it is about seeing and attacking all the things that are standing in our way. Yes, of course, it requires an ongoing acknowledgment, confession, and repentance of our sin. It also requires an ongoing journey into and through our stories. It is not for the faint of heart, but I promise you, the life that you are desperate for and have been looking for your entire life is right in front of you. I'm hoping that you will join the dangerous misfit militia of people who have relentlessly pursued it and found it. I'm hoping you will join me, join us, in changing what people think when they hear the word *Christian*. We do that one person at a time. It starts with you. Andy Stanley, in his book *Not in It to Win It*, asked a question that may be more important than ever today. He said, "Christianity was the catalyst for the most monumental cultural transformation our world has ever seen. Can it happen again?"[5] The answer is YES! God is waiting for each of us to say yes. R. T. Kendall warned that "sometimes the greatest opposition to what God wants to do next comes from those who were on the cutting edge of what God did last."[6] Let's not be those people. Let's rise up, join the militia, and pray. God has moved mountains in the past. Let's pray that he will use us to do it again. Father, use us to bring the rescue revolution that you want to bring to all people in the world around us.

A Hero Will Rise

So, what if your separation, divorce, relationship breakdown, unemployment, financial disaster, affair, battle with cancer, addiction, abortion, all the meltdowns and mistakes in your life don't limit you at all, but in fact uniquely qualify you to bring the kingdom difference that only you can bring? God says that he uses the foolish things of the world to shame the wise (1 Cor. 1:27), that his strength is demonstrated in our weakness (2 Cor. 12:7–10). Religion tries to convince us that our place is on the end of the bench. Jesus says, "Get in there. I have no bench. I need you in the game." We have to learn to say good-bye to and to kill the limitations that religion has placed on us.

I want to leave you with this. I have seen and experienced it in my own life and in the lives of thousands of others now. It is true. If it is true for me, it is true for you. There is no limit to what Jesus can do for you, in you, and through you. What unique kingdom mischief is God calling you up and into? Let's lock arms and do this! There is no limit to what God can do through us! Let's become the dangerous militia that he created us to be. Stay in your story, continue to experience the rescue of Jesus, and live to rescue others. Pursue life in all three of those circles, all the time. Let's finish our journey with this.

> Now to him who is able to do immeasurably more than all we ask or imagine, according to his power that is at work within us, to him be glory in the church and in Christ Jesus throughout all generations, for ever and ever! Amen. (Eph. 3:20–21)

More than we could ever ask or possibly imagine! Are you kidding me? What are we waiting for? My *Gladiator* poster says "A hero will rise." That hero, my friend, is you. Let's go!

A Note from Stacy

———◇———

Last week at church Greg once again mentioned our story. Our twenty-one-year-old daughter, Stella, who was sitting next to me, leaned over and whispered, "You don't seem fazed by this anymore" (eighteen years later). I wanted to whisper back, but it was during the service, so I waited until after. Do you know what I told her? I said, "No, I am not fazed by it, and here's why. I have a much better marriage now than so many people out there in the world today."

Obviously, that is not something I often say publicly, but it is true. And that is not because I have settled for less or lowered my expectations or standards. I have expected and continue to expect more of Greg every day. I can say that because Greg did *so* much work! There is no denying he did incredible damage to my heart and the hearts of our daughters. But despite my doubts about him, and living with the likelihood that our marriage was over, I had a front-row seat to watch him at work. For about three years a great counselor helped and guided him to figure out why he would ever have done that to me and our girls, the people he loved with all his heart.

When Greg talks about our story, he says Jesus and I are the heroes. Of course, Jesus is the real hero; all I did was make a daily decision to stay in the story. Yes, Greg and I were both broken people, but he went off the deep end. That daily decision was not easy. I was extremely skeptical. I had doubts, fears, times when it felt impossible, and honestly times when I wasn't sure that it was going to work. Despite that, Greg worked so hard that I was amazed. In counseling, he became aware of his story and brokenness, and began to chase hard after the healing, restoration, and redemption that he had learned were available to him. The jury was still out for me, and we weren't rushing to marital bliss and happily ever after, but I could not deny how hard he was working. It was obvious that nothing, absolutely nothing, was more important than becoming the husband and father that God had created him to be.

Despite my doubts, hesitations, and fears—and his less-than-perfect days along the way—I could not deny his determination to change, to become all that God created him to be. Boy did he heal! When our two oldest daughters were made aware of Greg's actions, it came as a huge shock to them. Despite his extreme brokenness, he had always been a great dad. With the help of Jesus and his counselor, Rob, Greg would become an even more amazing one. Over the past eighteen years, I've watched him intentionally go after the wounds he caused in each of our daughters' hearts and stories. He has pursued and continues to pursue our girls with a passion while never allowing his relationship with them to take precedence over his relationship with me.

Over the years, many people have asked me how I did it. The answer is one day at a time as Jesus gave me the strength. Greg was willing to take the long road and do the hard work—we both were. Please don't hear me say that he is now perfect. He's not and will never be. He's busy, and the challenges of leading a church in today's world are real. Sometimes, he can be a challenge to live with; I probably can be too. We still disagree, fight, and have days where we have had enough of each other. But our marriage, friendship, intimacy, and connection are better today than they have ever been. They continue to get better. He continues to stay in his story every day and allow Jesus to rescue him. While it took a long time to restore our marriage, I completely trust him.

Because of his self-awareness and his continuing hard work to pursue our daughters and me, now our sons-in-law and grandkids reap the benefits too. I love seeing Greg's relationship with our girls, their guys, and our grandkids. God's goodness continues in our story through our family as our girls and sons-in-law continue their own journeys of self-awareness and pursue and experience rescue and healing. We are now closing in on twenty years later and our family of eighteen is growing more relationally connected and stronger than we have ever been.

If you feel empathy and compassion as we share our story, thank you. If you have been on the receiving end of this kind of pain in your own story, I'm so sorry. If your story ended differently than mine, my heart goes out to you. Should you feel sorry for me? I would ask you not to. God has brought incredible healing to my heart and life. Regardless of how your story reads, there's hope for you. The same healing, redemption, and restoration are available to you. Whether we are on the giving or receiving end of the pain, the answer is the same. It's the journey that Greg charts out in this book: discovering the significance of our stories and beginning to experience Jesus in all of it.

My whole family is blessed. I truly believe that at a certain point God said, "No, Greg, I did not create you for this. I have bigger plans for you." Just as he promises, what the enemy intended to steal, kill, and destroy, God turned to good. Greg continues to speak to broken people every week. He is able to say "been there, done that, and there's hope." There's always hope in Jesus. Every week, people who have things in their lives that they wish they could change and do over, people who have hurt people and been hurt by people, even the people that they love the most, are experiencing the rescue of Jesus. Broken people are beginning to understand that despite how their stories read, God loves them no matter what.

Yes, my story with Greg has left scars, but some terrible, ugly, heart-wrenching, and devastating chapters have ultimately led to an incredibly beautiful story. A story that, despite it all, every day, I love living.

Acknowledgments

———◆———

I would like to express my deepest gratitude to everyone who has played a role in bringing *The Rest of Your Story* to the world. First and foremost, I want to acknowledge and thank my beautiful wife, Stacy, who is my hero and has been fearless in our journey together over the past forty years. There is no story without you. I am also so grateful for my family: my four daughters Sydney, Sloane, Spencer, and Stella, my sons-in-law Keith, Ethan, and Mike, and the boyfriend Aizik who is a keeper too. You each follow Jesus in a unique, beautiful, and contagious way. I am so proud of who you are. Your love and belief in me inspire me and keep me in the fight every day. I could not have done this without you. To all of our growing tribe of grandkids: Decker, Maverick, Atticus, Hudson, Emma, Theodora, Graham, and growing, I love you with all my heart, am so thankful for you and proud of you. I hope this book becomes a source of hope and strength for you when

Pops is gone and life gets tough. To my dad and mom, Lee Roy and Janette Lindsey. Dad, it has been twenty years now since you passed away. I really miss you. Mom and Dad, thank you for making sure that I grew up to know Jesus. Despite all of my resistance and running along the way, I rely on all that I learned in those years in church every day. Thanks too for the unconditional love that you have always had for me. For my little sister Robin Walls, you have always been a pain, but thanks for never letting go of me even when I gave you reasons to. I also want to acknowledge and thank my Klapheke family: Bill, Cathy, Christy, Anne, Betsy, Brad, Leslie, and Meg. You could have written me off for crushing your sister's heart. You didn't. Thank you for never giving up on me/us.

To Michael Covington at David C Cook, thank you for seeing something in me, recognizing that this message needed to get out, pursuing me, and for your tireless work in advocating for me and this book. Your belief in my vision, leadership, and writing means the world to me. I want to thank my editors, Kevin Scott and Jack Campbell, who have worked with me so creatively to refine the manuscript. Your attention to detail and commitment to excellence truly made this book better. Thank you for your excitement about the book along the way too. To the entire publishing team at David C Cook, thank you for believing in me, saying yes, and for your commitment to helping me share this message with the world.

I also want to acknowledge my incredible team at Discovery Church, who continue to inspire me with their creativity, passion, fire, and dedication to story and rescue and making the world a better place. Our mission is anything but easy. Your support and encouragement have been a constant source of inspiration and strength. To all who have been a part of the DCC story, staff or elders, past or present, thank you for all you have done to move this much needed mission and vision forward. To my friends Kevin and Jean Butcher, Craig and Sheryl Dykema, Daryl and Vicky Collings, and Terry Anderson, doing life closely with you has been a game changer for Stacy and me. Thanks for being a safe place, for loving us like you do, and for always having our backs. To all of those not named (there are too many to mention) who have walked with me along the way at different points of this sixty-year journey, thank you for believing in me, inspiring me, pushing me, challenging me, teaching me, correcting me, loving me and for being a part of who I continue to become.

Finally, thank you to all those who read this book. My hope is that *The Rest of Your Story* will inspire and challenge you to see your life through an entirely new lens, to chase the healing, redemption, and restoration that Jesus wants to bring into your life, to embrace unconventional you, and to step up and into all that God created you to be. This world desperately needs who you were made to be. Strength and Honor!

Greg Lindsey

Notes

———◇———

Chapter 2: Point of Origin

1. Rick Pitino, *Success Is a Choice: Ten Steps to Overachieving in Business and Life* (New York: Broadway Books, 1998), 83.
2. Richard Rohr, *Things Hidden: Scripture as Spirituality* (Cincinnati, OH: Franciscan Media, 2022), ch. 1.

Chapter 3: The Only Easy Day Was Yesterday

1. John Eldredge, *Waking the Dead: The Secret to a Heart Fully Alive* (Nashville, TN: Thomas Nelson, 2003), 151.

Chapter 4: Buried Treasure

1. Morgan Snyder, *Becoming a King: The Path to Restoring the Heart of a Man* (Nashville, TN: Thomas Nelson, 2020), 108.
2. Snyder, *Becoming a King*, 96.

3. Brennan Manning, *Abba's Child: The Cry of the Heart for Intimate Belonging* (Colorado Springs: NavPress, 2015), 12.

4. John Eldredge, *Wild at Heart: Discovering the Secret of a Man's Soul* (Nashville, TN: Thomas Nelson, 2010), 50.

5. Reggie McNeal, *Practicing Greatness: 7 Disciplines of Extraordinary Spiritual Leaders* (San Francisco: Jossey-Bass, 2006), 11.

Chapter 6: Something to Prove

1. Jason Redman, *The Trident: The Forging and Reforging of a Navy SEAL Leader* (New York: William Morrow, 2013), 204.

2. Redman, *Trident*, 172.

3. Chandler Moore and Naomi Raine, "Jireh," *Elevation Worship+1*. Elevation Worship Records, 2021.

4. Jonathan Helser, "I am Your Beloved," *The Land I'm Livin' In (Live)*. Bethel Music, 2022.

Chapter 7: The Rest of the Story

1. Curt Thompson, *The Soul of Shame: Retelling the Stories We Tell about Ourselves* (Downers Grove, IL: IVP Books, 2015), 62.

2. Thompson, *Soul of Shame*, 179.

3. Morgan Snyder, "Restoring the True Man," *Become Good Soil Podcast*, episode 108, May 10, 2022.

Chapter 8: Different

1. Debra Hirsch, *Redeeming Sex: Naked Conversations about Sexuality and Spirituality* (Downers Grove, IL: IVP Books, 2015), 31, 120.

2. Gregory A. Boyd, *The Myth of a Christian Nation: How the Quest for Political Power Is Destroying the Church* (Grand Rapids, MI: Zondervan, 2009), 48.

3. Preston Sprinkle, *Embodied: Transgender Identities, the Church, and What the Bible Has to Say* (Colorado Springs: David C Cook, 2021), 27.

Chapter 9: Embracing Unconventional You

1. Morgan Snyder, *Becoming a King: The Path to Restoring the Heart of a Man* (Nashville, TN: Thomas Nelson, 2020), 93.

2. A. W. Tozer, *The Pursuit of God* (Mansfield Centre, CT: Martino, 2009), 127.

3. Stephen Mansfield, *The Search for God and Guinness: A Biography of the Beer That Changed the World* (Nashville, TN: Thomas Nelson, 2009), 43.

4. Mark Batterson, *Win the Day: 7 Daily Habits to Help You Stress Less and Accomplish More* (Colorado Springs: Multnomah, 2020), 34.

5. Martin Luther King Jr., as quoted by The Martin Luther King Jr. Center, Twitter post, October 25, 2020, 11:40 a.m., https://twitter .com/thekingcenter/status/1320389731532800000?lang=en.

Chapter 10: Finding Tonto

1. John Eldredge, *Wild at Heart: Discovering the Secret of a Man's Soul* (Nashville, TN: Thomas Nelson, 2010), 81.

Chapter 11: A Call to Action with a Sense of Urgency

1. Mark Batterson, *Chase the Lion: If Your Dream Doesn't Scare You, It's Too Small* (Colorado Springs: Multnomah, 2016), ix.

Chapter 12: A Dangerous Militia

1. Hugh Halter and Matt Smay, *The Tangible Kingdom: Creating Incarnational Community* (San Francisco: Jossey-Bass, 2008), 140.

2. Jason Redman, *The Trident: The Forging and Reforging of a Navy SEAL Leader* (New York: William Morrow, 2013), 468.

3. Redman, *Trident*, epigraph.

4. Alan Hirsch and Tim Catchim, *The Permanent Revolution: Apostolic Imagination and Practice for the 21st Century Church* (San Francisco: Jossey-Bass, 2012), loc. 6290.

5. Andy Stanley, *Not in It to Win It: Why Choosing Sides Sidelines the Church* (Grand Rapids, MI: Zondervan, 2022), 64.

6. R. T. Kendall, *The Anointing: Yesterday, Today, and Tomorrow* (Lake Mary, FL: Charisma House, 2003), 133.